CHILDHOOD ASTHMA:
Diagnosis, Treatment and Management

PRACTICAL PROBLEMS IN MEDICINE

CHILDHOOD ASTHMA:
Diagnosis, Treatment and Management

Anthony D Milner, MD, FRCP, DCH
Professor of Paediatric Respiratory Medicine,
University of Nottingham

MARTIN DUNITZ

First published in the United Kingdom in 1987
by Martin Dunitz Ltd, 154 Camden High Street,
London NW1 0NE

British Library Cataloguing in Publication Data

Milner, Anthony D.
  Practical management of childhood asthma.
  —(Practical problems in medicine)
  1. Asthma in children
  I. Title   II. Series
  618.92′238   RJ436.A8

  ISBN 0–948269–02–2

Phototypeset by Scribe Design, Gillingham, Kent
Printed and bound in Singapore by Toppan Printing Company (S) Pte Ltd

To Ben who was beautiful in his way, and to HS who is certainly beautiful in hers

Acknowledgments

I wish to acknowledge my great debt to Chris Fensom for her help in the preparation of this manuscript and to Mrs Osborne for providing the very graphic parents' story. I would also like to thank Stephen Alexander, Cherene Bowler, Neil Creasey and Sarah Rudd for allowing their photographs to be included in the text.

1987   A.D.M.

The diagrams were drawn by Pantek Graphics, Maidstone.

Contents

	Acknowledgments	vi
1	Definition and natural history of childhood asthma	1
2	Bronchoconstriction	7
3	Measurement of lung function	18
4	Diagnosis	31
5	Drug treatment	43
6	Allergen avoidance and desensitization	69
7	The child and his asthma	78
8	Alternative therapies	85
9	Specific asthma problems	88
10	Management of an acute asthma attack	94
11	Management of childhood asthma in general practice *Dr Douglas Jenkinson*	109
12	Clinical case histories	120
	Appendix	130
	References	132
	Index	143

1
Definition and natural history of childhood asthma

WHAT IS ASTHMA?

Although it is generally agreed that asthma is a condition in which there is reversible airways obstruction, it remains impossible to reach universal consensus on a precise definition which can be applied to all.[1] This is particularly a problem in children. We have, for example, many children who have recurrent wheezing and coughing attacks in the first year of life who do not respond to bronchodilator drugs. They are often described as having wheezy bronchitis, but follow-up studies have shown that these children are indistinguishable from older asthmatic children and respond normally to antiasthma therapy once they are over the age of fifteen months.[2]

In an attempt to get round these problems, wide-ranging studies have been carried out to define asthma in terms of abnormal airways lability. This can be investigated with a number of different challenges including exercise or inhaled cold air, ultrasonic nebulized water, histamine or methacholine. Epidemiological studies have shown that by using these techniques groups of children can be characterized according to their responses. Unfortunately the correlation between abnormal airways lability as measured by these techniques and the pattern of clinically obvious asthma symptoms in individual children is not close. There are some children who have greatly enhanced airways lability and yet no symptoms, while others who have responses within the normal range have recurrent attacks of coughing, wheezing and breathlessness (see Figure 1.1).[3] A further problem is that airways lability varies with time. It has recently been demonstrated that exposure to inhaled allergens can considerably increase sensitivity to histamine for several weeks.[4] There is also good evidence that damage to the airways produces abnormal airways lability whether this be due to a viral infection, such as influenza or respiratory syncytial virus (RSV) bronchiolitis, *Mycoplasma pneumoniae*, a foreign body or even drowning.[5] Although this increased sensitivity is only temporary, many of the children have attacks of bronchoconstriction which respond to antiasthma therapy and to my mind should be included within the asthma spectrum. Nevertheless the studies on airways lability have been of considerable interest and they support the concept that though there may be genetic influences at work, asthma represents one end of a continuous spectrum rather than a specific defect, such as cystic fibrosis (see Figure 1.2).

For the purpose of this book, the diagnosis of asthma will be used for all children up to

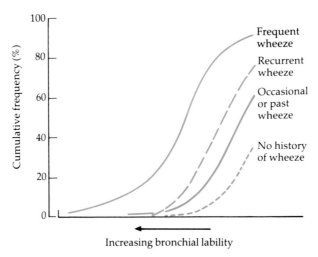

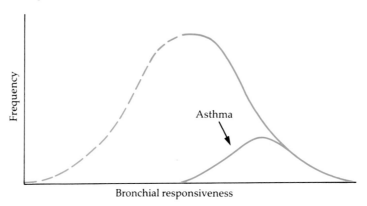

Figure 1.1 Although children with the most severe symptoms tend to have most bronchial lability, there is considerable overlap.

Figure 1.2 Asthma represents the end of a spectrum.

the age of sixteen years who have symptoms secondary to bronchoconstriction which, either in the short term or the long term, respond to antiasthma therapy.

AETIOLOGY AND NATURAL HISTORY OF ASTHMA

Although our knowledge of the biochemical, cellular, and physiological changes which occur in asthma has improved dramatically, we still have difficulty providing parents with the satisfactory answer to the question, 'Why does our child have asthma?' In the UK each year and probably in all other Caucasian countries, approximately 10 per cent of children will have symptoms of coughing and wheezing due to an abnormal airways lability. By the age of ten, at least 20 per cent of children will at some time have had symptoms due to an underlying asthma.[3] Although secure data are difficult to obtain, it is likely that the incidence of asthma is at least as high in all children of European descent. The incidence in children born in India, in Papua New Guinea and to native

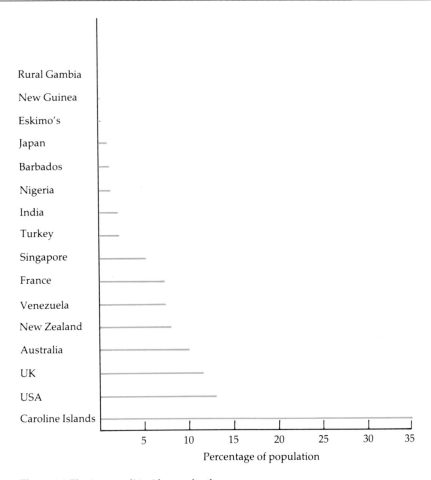

Rural Gambia
New Guinea
Eskimo's
Japan
Barbados
Nigeria
India
Turkey
Singapore
France
Venezuela
New Zealand
Australia
UK
USA
Caroline Islands

5   10   15   20   25   30   35

Percentage of population

Figure 1.3 The 'reported' incidence of asthma.

Indian and Eskimo families in North America, however, is much lower (see Figure 1.3). The incidence in Indian children born in the UK appears to be at least as high as in Caucasian children born in the UK.[6] Certainly, no race is immune from this condition, and some are particularly susceptible. An example of this is provided by the population of Tristan da Cunha, a highly inbred and relatively isolated community which was started by fifteen settlers from Holland. A study in 1946 showed that a high proportion of the population, over 45 per cent, had asthma. This provides strong support for the concept that asthma is, at least in part, genetically determined. The fact that boys are more than twice as likely as girls to have asthma also favours a genetic influence, even though this difference disappears in adult life. Further data are provided by recent epidemiological studies which have shown that if both parents have asthma, there is a 40 per cent chance that each of their children will have asthma symptoms at some time in childhood. If only one parent is affected this falls to approximately 25 per cent.

Studies do not, however, indicate that asthma is inherited on Mendelian lines. The possibilities are either that it is inherited on a multifactorial basis, along the lines of hare-lip and cleft palate, or that environmental factors are also important. Of these, respiratory tract infections are the most obvious. Empey and his colleagues[7] have provided strong evidence that lower respiratory tract infections due to the influenza virus create abnormal airways lability in previously non-asthmatic subjects. These changes, documented by histamine challenges, persist for several weeks. There is evidence that this occurs in childhood as well.[8] In addition, there are now a number of studies showing that babies who have acute viral bronchiolitis of sufficient severity to require admission to hospital will often have recurrent attacks of coughing and wheezing for the next three to five years.[9] Studies have shown that five years and ten years after the acute episode, the prevalence of asthma symptoms is still higher than in the control population (30 per cent and 16 per cent respectively) and an increased proportion have abnormal airways lability which can be demonstrated either by exercise or histamine challenge.[10] It is possible that RSV infection leads to severe symptoms in those predestined to develop asthma. This concept is given some support by the finding that babies mildly affected (ie, not requiring hospital admission) are less likely to have symptoms or abnormal airways lability seven years later.[11] The evidence against this is that the prevalence of asthma symptoms in the siblings of babies requiring admission to hospital with acute bronchiolitis is no different from that in the general population.[10] There is also no evidence of an association with a family history of atopy or indeed skin tests in this particular group of babies, a very different pattern from that seen in the general asthmatic population.[9,10] These findings throw the balance of evidence in favour of the concept that it is the RSV infection which is producing abnormal airways lability in children who are not particularly predisposed to asthma.[11]

It has been calculated that approximately 20 per cent of all wheezing attacks in the first five years of life are the result of previous attacks of acute bronchiolitis. There are also some data indicating that a similar, though milder and shorter-lasting, effect can be produced by *Mycoplasma pneumoniae* infections.[12]

Although hard data are difficult to obtain, paediatricians in New Zealand have little doubt that both the incidence and severity of childhood asthma has increased considerably over the last ten years.[13] The reasons for this remains obscure, but many suspect that environmental factors are responsible for these changes.

Allergy

The relationship between an atopic tendency and childhood asthma remains in dispute. The large majority of asthmatic children have atopy. This is usually defined as 'an untoward physiological event mediated by a variety of different immunologic reactions'[14] and in practice represents a Type I IgE mediated reaction. Many of these children have or have had eczema at some time in the past. Most have hay fever symptoms, with deterioration of their asthma when the grass or tree pollens are abundant. Some give dramatic histories indicating severe sensitivity to animal fur, house dust or even foods. However, over 50 per cent of children who have a strong allergic tendency, for example, eczema, never have any asthma symptoms and, as already described, a considerable number wheeze after viral infections and yet have no apparent allergic triggers. It is now generally agreed that allergy is inherited as a Mendelian dominant with variable expression and probably affects between 30 and 40 per cent of the population.[15] This suggests that at some time an allergic tendency provided a survival benefit, although the nature of this remains obscure. There is also some evidence that environmental factors, including exposure to cow's milk in infancy, may bring out a latent atopic tendency.[16] The most attractive hypothesis is that abnormal airways lability is an acquired characteristic but that those with an inherited atopic tendency have an increased susceptibility. This raises the exciting concept that it may be possible to block environmental triggers in the future and thus eliminate asthma either by preventing contact with allergen triggers in infancy[17] or by immunizing babies or even pregnant mothers against infective agents such as RSV.

Outcome

The second question parents usually ask is, 'Will my child grow out of his symptoms?' Again it is impossible to give more than a statistical probability based on what epidemiological evidence is available. The best information on the outcome of asthma in childhood comes from the Melbourne study.[18,19] The investigators recruited over two hundred children with wheezing attacks at the age of seven years and have since reassessed them at seven-year intervals:

- At the age of fourteen years
  —over 70 per cent of those with mild or occasional symptoms were symptom free;
  —20 per cent of those with severe or chronic symptoms were symptom free.
- At the age of twenty-one years
  —30 per cent of those who had become asymptomatic at age fourteen were coughing and wheezing again.[20]

There remain two particular problems with these data. First, they give us no information on the natural history of asthma in the first seven years of life; and second, they give us no information on the natural history of wheezing commencing after the age of seven years. Nevertheless the data can be used to help provide many parents with at least some answers to their question. There are also studies examining the outcome of children wheezing in the first few years of life in association with viral infections, who had largely been labelled as having wheezy bronchitis. These studies have shown that 70 per cent of those with symptoms at the age of two to three years will have improved or lost their symptoms by the age of seven years.[10] There are now a number of epidemiological studies on the natural history of wheezing and coughing after bronchiolitis, indicating that 80 per cent will have symptoms in the two years after the acute attack,[9] but of these less than half will still have symptoms by the time they reach the age of five years and less than 20 per cent by the age of ten years.[10]

It is therefore reasonable to take a positive approach and reassure parents that childhood asthma tends to improve with time, that those wheezing without obvious allergic triggers in the first few years of life may well be asymptomatic by the age of six or seven years and even those with obvious atopy are likely to improve by or during adolescence.

Death in asthma

A further question occasionally asked but often considered by parents is 'Will my child die in an asthma attack?' A very positive answer can be given because, as the figures below will demonstrate, mortality in childhood is far lower than it is in the adult population:

- Approximately 1500 people die each year in the UK as a direct result of their asthma, (ie, 1 in 30000 of the total population) giving an annual risk rate of about 1 in 2000 of all asthmatic patients.

- In the first five years of life, only four to seven children die from asthma, a rate of between 1 and 2 per 100000 wheezing preschool children.

- Although the mortality rate rises through childhood, only approximately fifty of the original 1500 deaths occur under the age of fifteen years. This gives an annual death rate of approximately 1 in 20000 of asthmatic children, assuming that 10 per cent of the population are asthmatic. This is approximately one tenth of the mortality rate experienced by the adult asthmatic population.

Although deaths do occur in children whose asthma is considered to be intermittent and not particularly severe, the majority occur in those who have persistent chronic symptoms. Even in this group, the chances of death, although present and tragic, are very small.

PRACTICAL POINTS

- Asthma is best defined as a condition in which there is abnormal (increased) airways lability.

- Asthma occurs twice as often in boys as in girls and has a prevalence of approximately 10 per cent. Twenty per cent of children will have had asthma symptoms by the age of ten years.

- Although atopic children are more likely to have asthma, many do not, and conversely there are many in childhood who wheeze with viral infections and who are not atopic.

- Evidence suggests that atopy is inherited while abnormal airways lability is largely acquired.

- There is a tendency towards improvement in childhood asthma, although some relapse in adult life. Mortality, although a major worry, is fortunately rare.

2
Bronchoconstriction

THE HEALTHY STATE

In health, resistance to airflow is determined largely by anatomical factors which are modified by physiological influences. In infancy and early childhood, the diameter of the large airways is considerably less than that encountered in adult life so the resistance to airflow is inevitably higher (see Table 2.1). However, there is an inverse relationship

Table 2.1 Diameter of the airways (mm) (from Silverman M, '*Asthma in childhood*', Current Medical Literature Ltd.)

	Infant	Child (Aged 6–8 yrs)	Adult
Trachea	5	10	16
Bronchioles	0.4	0.5	0.7
Alveoli	0.07	0.15	0.3

between the increase in resting lung volume (functional residual capacity) and the fall in resistance as lung growth occurs (see Figure 2.1). The physiological influence primarily responsible for modifying airway diameter in health is that of the autonomic system. In health, a mild degree of bronchoconstriction is maintained by the parasympathetic (vagal) system which liberates acetylcholine at the nerve endings. The airways also contain sympathetic nerve endings which may either act directly on smooth muscle or modify ganglionic function in the airway walls. There are both alpha and beta receptor sites on the smooth muscle which, when stimulated, lead to bronchoconstriction and bronchodilatation respectively. Even the healthiest of children show some bronchodilatation on receiving beta$_2$ stimulants, whereas beta$_2$ blocking agents do not seem to produce any obvious effect. This suggests that the system is not contributing particularly to bronchodilatation at rest, although at times of stress there is possibly a useful response to circulating catecholamines. We have little information on the importance of the alpha receptors in the balance of muscle tone in childhood (see Figure 2.2).

There is a third autonomic system, the non-adrenergic inhibitory or purinergic system,[1] the role of which has yet to be investigated in childhood.

Although advertising literature put out by the manufacturers of bronchodilator drugs would suggest that increased smooth muscle tone is the sole cause of bronchoconstriction, we know that the effective lumen of the airways is also determined by the degree of

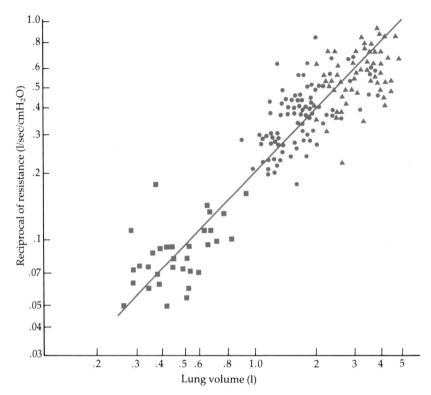

Figure 2.1 There is a direct relationship between lung volume and the reciprocal of resistance throughout childhood.

mucosal oedema and the presence of secretions and cellular debris within the airways themselves. This has to be taken into account in planning the most appropriate therapy.

Constriction of the smooth muscle surrounding the airways

The smooth muscle is influenced by hormones carried in the blood (adrenaline), mediators produced by the mast cells within the lung and from the macrophages, eosinophils, neutrophils and platelets, and finally by neural reflexes which produce both bronchodilatation (sympathetic) and bronchoconstriction (parasympathetic).

Mucosal oedema

This too is influenced by blood-borne hormones, neural reflexes and locally released mediators.

Collections of secretions

These are produced both by neural reflexes and by local release of mediators, and they include debris from within the airways.

Cilial activity has an important part to play in clearing secretions and debris from within the lungs. In asthma the epithelium is often damaged, inevitably interfering with cilial efficiency and further contributing to the pooling of secretions within the lungs.

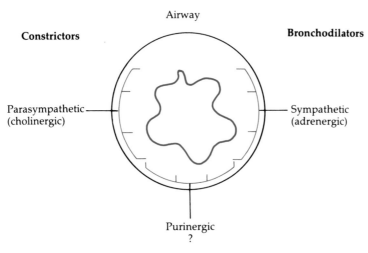

Figure 2.2 The autonomic nervous system of the lung.

MECHANISMS OF BRONCHOCONSTRICTION

There are several triggers which have been used to produce bronchoconstriction in the laboratory. These have taught us a great deal about the mechanisms and cellular changes involved in asthma attacks.

Histamine challenge

The bronchoconstrictor response to histamine has been used extensively to investigate and assess airways lability. A number of techniques have been developed, but the one most in favour is that of Chai.[2] The child's lung function is measured using either a peak flow meter or a simple spirometer from which a timed expiratory force of volume is derived. The child then takes three deep breaths from a jet nebulizer containing a weak solution of histamine phosphate (0.01 mg/ml), and the lung function is measured again 2 min later. This procedure is repeated using increasing concentrations of histamine, usually 0.1, 0.3, 1, 3 and 6 mg/ml until lung function falls by at least 20 per cent (see Figure 2.3). The correlation between response and asthma severity is not absolute. But a tendency for histamine sensitivity to be increased (ie, for lung function to fall at more dilute concentrations) indicates that there is an abnormal sensitivity of the smooth muscle, and probably also of the mucosa, to respond to stimuli.

Methacholine challenge

In some studies, methacholine[3] or even carbachol has been substituted for histamine. These cholinergic agents act on the parasympathetic nerve endings among the smooth muscles and the enhanced response to those compounds is again thought to reflect an abnormal airways lability rather than an enhanced parasympathetic effect in asthma. But it does indicate that vagal tone may be an important factor in an attack of bronchoconstriction.

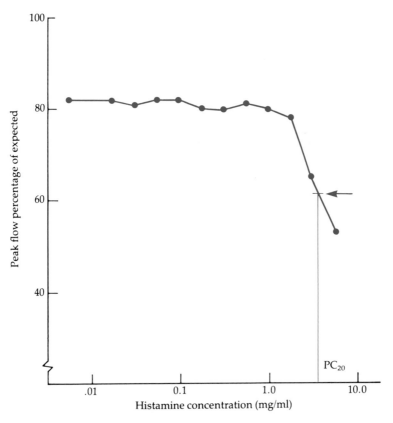

Figure 2.3 An example of a histamine challenge.

Exercise

Although it has been known for many centuries that exercise brings on bronchoconstriction in asthmatic children, the mechanism by which this occurs remains uncertain. The standard technique is to exercise the child submaximally for up to 6 min and measure the percentage fall in peak flow or forced expiratory volume at 2–5 min intervals for the next 15–20 min.[4] The heart rate at the end of exercise should exceed 170/min. A positive response (ie, a fall of peak flow greater than 15 per cent or a fall greater than 10 per cent in forced expiratory volume in 1 s (FEV_1)) occurs in over 80 per cent of asthmatic children. If the test is repeated on two or three different occasions, the response rate rises to over 95 per cent. If measurements are obtained at 1 min intervals during the exercise, it is also possible to show a rise in lung function at 1–2 min.[4] This may be due either to the release of catecholamines or to the withdrawal of vagal tone. The bronchoconstrictor response can be rapidly eliminated by inhaling beta₂ stimulants.[5] Prior treatment with sodium cromoglycate is usually effective in blocking the response, but not as effective as beta₂ stimulants. The effect of prior treatment with oral theophylline or inhaled cholinergic blocking agents is less dramatic. Inhaled topical or systemic steroids are ineffective, although longterm treatment (ie, more than six weeks) may reduce the response (see Figure 2.4).

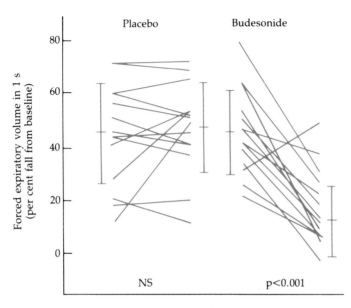

Figure 2.4 The fall in FEV$_1$ on exercise is unchanged after three weeks on placebo. Budesonide inhalations, however, radically reduce exercise-induced bronchoconstriction.

It is also well established that the bronchoconstrictor response depends on the type of exercise undertaken. The most effective is free running, followed by running first a treadmill and then a bicycle ergometer. Swimming in a heated pool is least likely to produce exercise-induced bronchoconstriction (EIB).[6] Recent studies[7] have shown that the EIB is due to the effects of inhaling relatively dry and cold air rather than to the metabolic changes produced by the exercise itself. Measurements of oesophageal temperature have shown that the temperature of the mediastinum falls by several degrees during prolonged exercise.[8] The development of cold air techniques for inducing bronchoconstriction has supported the idea that the response is due to this cooling effect. Careful studies by Sandy Anderson and her co-workers[9] have suggested, however, that it is the humidity of the air rather than the temperature which is important. Inhaling dry air at any temperature will have the effect of drying up the airway secretions and thus increasing the osmotic pressure. It is unlikely that this acts directly on the smooth muscle, as chemical mediators including neutrophil chemotactic factor and histamine have been found in the plasma of patients after prolonged exercise. This suggests that mast cell degranulation is involved. Additional support for this comes both from the protective effect of sodium cromoglycate and from the finding that there is a refractory period after exercise (ie, the fall in lung function is reduced or abolished in exercise tests repeated at 30–60 min).[10] This phenomenon does not occur after provocation by histamine or methacholine.

Cold air

The number of studies on the bronchoconstrictor response to cold air in children is limited.[11] The technique usually involves measuring lung function (peak flow or FEV) before and 5 min after hyperventilating cold air (-15 to $-18°C$) that contains sufficient carbon dioxide to maintain end tidal levels of 35–45 mmHg. As stated above, it is likely that the cold air is acting primarily by drying airway secretions and increasing osmotic gradients.

Ultrasonically nebulized distilled water

For many years distilled water was given to children as an ultrasonically nebulized mist on the assumption that this would help clear secretions from the lungs. Recent work has shown, however, that water delivered in this way is a potent bronchoconstrictor agent. The principle of the technique is to measure the response to inhalation of increasing volumes of distilled water and to note the volume that produces a 20 per cent fall in lung function. The mechanism inducing bronchoconstriction, thought to occur solely in asthmatic subjects, appears to be the reverse of that occurring on inhaling dry cold air (ie, the deposition of hypotonic solutions in the airways is producing osmotic shifts in the opposite direction). The main problem with this technique is that the ultrasonic mist is an irritant and tends to produce coughing, but this sensation does wear off. It may be that this will be a useful test for distinguishing those with abnormal airways lability.[12]

Allergen challenge

Although atopy is by no means universal in asthmatic children, many have attacks of asthma brought on by inhaling allergens, such as house dust, house dust mite, pollen moulds and animal dander. If weak solutions of these allergens are inhaled in sensitive patients, a fall in airways calibre will occur in 2–5 min. We know that this represents a Type I immune response, the allergen combining with antibody (IgE) attached to the mast cells within the airways. This induces the release of bronchoconstrictor agents from the mast cell granules, and these agents include histamine, neutral proteases such as tryptase, and chemotactic chemicals which act on eosinophils and neutrophils. The reaction with the mast cell also triggers the generation of new compounds including leukotrienes (slow-reacting substances of anaphylaxis, SRSA) particularly LTC_4, LTD_4 and LTE_4. The mast cells also synthesize prostaglandins (PGD_2) and a platelet-activating factor.[13] Whether each mast cell can produce the total range of chemicals or whether there is some specialization in function remains unclear, as does the role and relative importance of each of these compounds in the bronchoconstrictor response. One problem is that, with the exception of histamine, we do not have safe antagonists which can be used to treat the patient to see to what extent this modifies the response. Our information comes primarily from in vivo experiments on cell culture but also from the measurement of histamine and metabolites of prostaglandins, platelet factor and chemotactic chemicals in the blood of patients after allergen challenge.

The bronchoconstrictor response following antigen challenge reaches a peak within 15–20 min and then usually settles by 2–3 hours. Some children may show a second bronchoconstrictor response 4–8 hours later,[14] and this reaction, the so-called late response, tends to be more severe, lasts longer and responds far less dramatically to bronchodilator drugs. There is good evidence that the late response leads to an increase in bronchial reactivity as measured by histamine sensitivity lasting for weeks.[15] It was originally thought that this represented a Type III immunological response (ie, an interaction between antigen and antibody (IgG) in the serum with the consumption of complement). There is no evidence to support this suggestion, however, and current theories suggest that this secondary response is due either to an influx of inflammatory cells including neutrophils and eosinophils attracted by the chemotactic factors, or to the release of further chemicals from platelets aggregating within the lung. How the inflammatory cells would cause this secondary response has not yet been determined, but bronchial lavage after antigen challenge in asthmatic subjects has demonstrated that inflammatory cells do accumulate within the lung.

A further possible mechanism is that the immediate action loosens the junction between epithelial cells, allowing allergens to reach mast cells deeper in the airway walls.

Whatever the mechanism, the late response models severe asthma closely and can be totally blocked by prior treatment with corticosteroids.

SITE OF BRONCHOCONSTRICTION

There remains some dispute about the main site of airways obstruction although, for reasons discussed below, it seems probable that the large and small airways are both involved.

Although airways become progressively smaller towards the periphery of the lung, their number greatly increases so that the total cross-sectional area actually rises (see Figure 2.5). This means that the rate of flow of air is much slower in the small airways than in the major bronchi and trachea. Wheezing will only occur when the flow is turbulent (rough) and not when the flow is laminar (smooth and organized). Although the diameter of the tube down which air is flowing is important in defining the point at which turbulence starts, so too is the flow rate. This point of conversion occurs when the Reynolds number exceeds 2000, a condition only achieved in the trachea and large airways. The presence of a wheeze therefore indicates that bronchoconstriction is occurring in the large airways.

The model of the cross-sectional area of the airways illustrated in Figure 2.5 applies only over the normal tidal range. On full inspiration, the pattern will be exaggerated. As residual volume is approached, there is a progressive closure of the small airways as the pressure around the lungs (the intrapleural pressure) rises and the intraluminal pressure from the elastic recoil of the lungs progressively falls (see Figure 2.6). Thus the contribution of the small airways to the resistance rises to above that of the large airways as the child breathes out forcibly. At residual volume, all the small airways are closed and the peripheral resistance approaches infinity. If there are bronchoconstrictor changes in the small airways, airways closure will commence at higher lung volumes, and the volume at which total closure occurs will also be increased (ie, the lungs will be hyperinflated). So the presence of hyperinflation indicates that small airways are also involved. If the small-airways component is high relative to that of the large airways, the child will be hyperinflated, often without obvious wheezing. This mechanism also explains the situation in which the asthmatic child has a relatively quiet chest at times when the asthma is particularly severe: the peripheral airways obstruction is so severe that the child is unable to generate sufficient turbulence in the large airways to produce noise.

The hyperinflation is exacerbated by a second factor, that of dynamic compression.

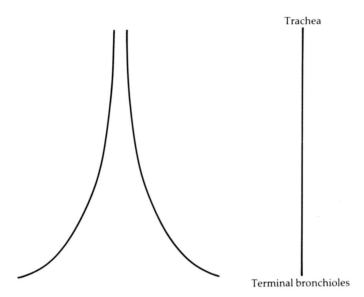

Figure 2.5 The increase in total cross-sectional area of all the airways progressing from the trachea to the terminal bronchioles.

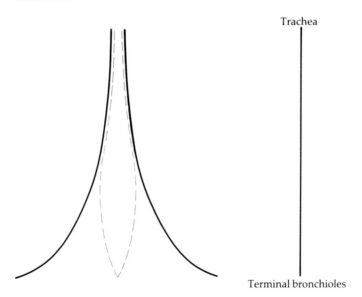

Figure 2.6 The total cross-sectional area of the airways during quiet breathing and on forced expiration to residual volume (dotted line).

On breathing in, the asthmatic child develops large negative intrathoracic pressures which tend to pull the airways open, thus reducing the airways obstruction. On expiration, the corresponding positive pressure produced by the accessory muscles tends to compress the airways, increasing the resistance (see Figure 2.7). This explains why at the beginning of an asthma attack it is more difficult for the child to breathe out

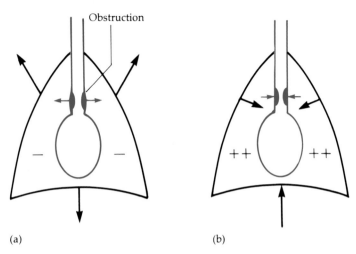

(a)   (b)

Figure 2.7 On inspiration (a) the negative intrathoracic pressures developed tend to pull the airways open, reducing the obstruction. On expiration (b), the positive pressures have the opposite effect.

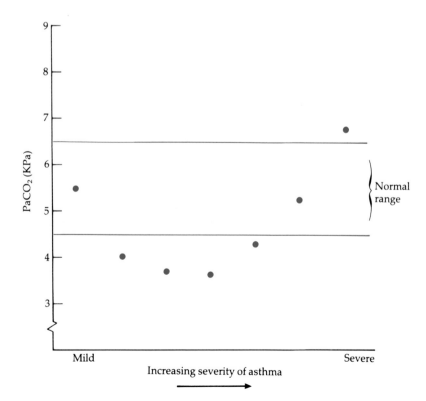

Figure 2.8 Carbon dioxide and asthma.

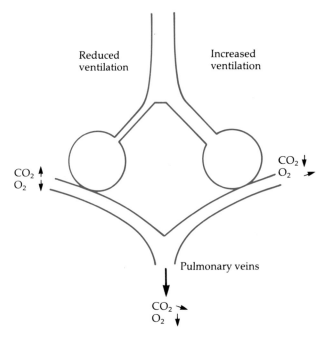

Figure 2.9 Blood leaving poorly ventilated units will be desaturated and have increased CO_2 levels. Blood from units with increased ventilation will have reduced CO_2 levels but normal or only slightly increased O_2 levels. The overall effect is for blood in the pulmonary vein to be desaturated but to have low or normal CO_2 levels.

than to breathe in. The effect of this imbalance is that the time constant (ie, the time for 63 per cent of the volume change to occur) is considerably longer on expiration than on inspiration. This has the effect of pumping the lung up to a higher volume, which has two advantages to the asthmatic: firstly, at higher lung volumes the airways will tend to receive greater support, and secondly, the lung parenchyma will be stretched so that during expiration the alveolar pressure will be raised by the elastic recoil. As the pressure is transmitted proximally this will also tend to hold open the airways. To achieve this the child has to work harder on inspiration in order to gain these benefits on the next breath out. This transference of work is clearly apparent to children, who if asked will often say that in a severe attack of asthma it is breathing in which is a problem rather than breathing out!

EFFECTS ON BLOOD GASES

The changes described above, including increases in peripheral airways obstruction and hyperinflation, are not homogeneous but affect different areas of the lungs to different extents. The effect of this is that the compliance and time constants of the different units will vary considerably, so that during the time available on inspiration and expiration some will receive relatively little fresh air while others that are less affected will actually have more ventilation than usual. The sensation of airways obstruction causes the child to hyperventilate until either he becomes exhausted or very severe asthma is present. As the arterial carbon dioxide level is directly related to alveolar ventilation, this will initially fall (see Figure 2.8) but then begin to climb again if the airways obstruction becomes progressively worse and alveolar ventilation begins to fall. For this reason even a normal arterial carbon dioxide level is regarded as a sign of severe airways obstruction in the course of an asthma attack, and even a modest increase above normal (4.5–6.5 kPa) is often considered as an indication for supportive ventilation in the near future (see page 106).

The pattern of changes in arterial oxygen tension is different, due to the mechanism of transport as oxyhaemoglobin. There are local vasoactive reflexes which tend to alter alveolar blood flow to match changes in ventilation. These are imperfect. Thus, although the blood flow to poorly ventilated alveoli will fall, the blood supply will still tend to exceed the optimal match. So blood leaving that alveolus will contain perhaps 12 ml of oxygen per 100 ml of blood, of which approximately 0.4 ml will be in solution and the remainder in combination with haemoglobin. Well-ventilated units may have an increased blood supply, but once the haemoglobin-carrying capacity reaches saturation (22 ml/100 ml) only the solution component can increase. As this is relatively small, the saturation in the mixed pulmonary venous blood will inevitably be considerably less than 100 per cent, even when the minute ventilation has greatly increased (see Figure 2.9). Thus the saturation drop is solely a reflection of small-airways involvement with the ventilation:perfusion mismatch until the asthma is so severe that the child is unable to maintain an adequate ventilation and the arterial carbon dioxide levels start to rise.

PRACTICAL POINTS

- In health, the airways are mildly constricted by parasympathetic activity.

- In asthma, bronchoconstriction is produced by smooth muscle spasm, mucosal oedema and intraluminal secretions. Epithelial damage will reduce cilial clearance.

- Bronchial lability can be assessed by inhaling histamine, methacholine, carbachol, ultrasonically nebulized distilled water and exercise. Allergen challenge acts by leading to the liberation of mediators from several cell types including mast cells in the respiratory tract, and can also produce a late reaction which more closely models asthma attacks.

- Bronchoconstriction leads to hyperinflation which increases the work needed to inhale, but aids expiration.

- Arterial oxygen levels fall early; carbon dioxide levels also fall early but rise as the obstruction progresses.

3
Measurement of lung function

Perception of the severity of symptoms by asthmatic children and their parents is notoriously variable; some become acutely anxious about relatively trivial attacks, while others almost ignore severe chronic airways obstruction. The ability of the doctor to assess the degree of obstruction from clinical examination is also often unimpressive. Lung function tests, although themselves imperfect, do provide an objective measurement which can prevent erroneous decisions based on an inappropriate assessment of severity. The lung function tests are also of considerable value in the diagnosis of abnormal airways lability (asthma) and are essential in research, allowing us to assess response to new therapy and also to increase our understanding of the pathophysiological changes occurring in asthma.

Although it is possible to measure the degree of airways obstruction directly, the techniques are relatively difficult and require expensive equipment. For this reason, information on the state of the airways is usually derived from the secondary effects of the obstruction. As young children need to be approached differently, schoolchildren (five years and over) will be considered first, then those between the ages of three and five years, and finally those in the first two to three years of life. Normal data are now available for all measurements. These are almost always related to height. This is in general a satisfactory solution, but problems arise once growth has slowed in adolescence because lung function continues to rise, particularly in males (see Figure 3.1). Data to be available soon will include other criteria, such as age and pubertal staging.

SCHOOLCHILDREN (FIVE YEARS AND UPWARDS)

Peak expiratory flow rate (PEFR)

If children are encouraged to fill their lungs and then breathe out as hard and as fast as they can, the expiratory flow rate will rise rapidly to a peak and then fall. The maximum flow which is maintained for 10 ms is defined as the PEFR. This flow rate is determined both by the diameter of the airways at their narrowest point and by the intrathoracic pressure which the child generates with the help of his accessory respiratory muscles. Devices available to measure the PEFR include the original Wright's peak flow meter and more recent developments (see Figure 3.2). All have spring-loaded systems, with either vanes or pistons which are deflected by the impact of the child's expired air. A simple and less accurate substitute is a whistle device in which air is allowed to leak away.

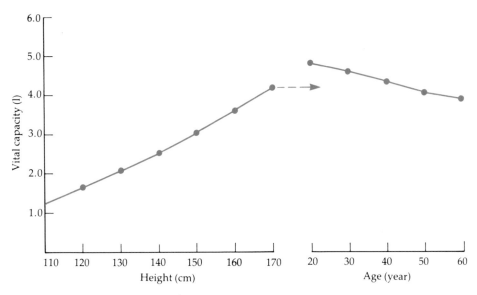

Figure 3.1 Lung function, such as vital capacity, is closely related to height up to the time of adolescence but then it increases after growth has stopped. In adult life there is a slow deterioration.

Figure 3.2 A selection of devices for measuring peak flow in the clinic or ward.

The advantages of the PEFR are that the apparatus required is relatively inexpensive, requires little patient training, is regarded as fun by the children and is reasonably reproducible (coefficient of variation approximately 10 per cent).[1] The disadvantages are that unrepresentatively low values will be obtained if the child does not exert his maximal expiratory efforts, and the forced expiratory effort greatly increases the tendency for dynamic compression, producing results which do not correlate closely with measurements during quiet breathing.

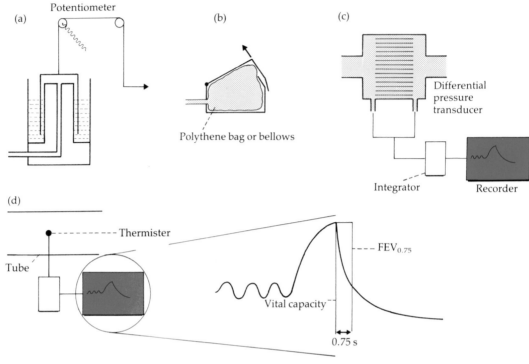

Figure 3.3 Devices for measuring volumes.

Timed forced expiratory volume (FEV)

Another time-honoured method for assessing obstruction is to measure the volume of air that can be forcibly expired in a set time, usually 1 s, the FEV_1. The volume can be measured using either a water spirometer or a dry spirometer, such as the Vitalograph. These measurements can also be obtained from devices, such as pneumotachographs, which measure the flow rate. Volume is then derived by electronically integrating flow against time. There are now a number of other devices, either using heater wires cooled by the flow of air or based on the venturi effect (see Figure 3.3). All these systems are adequately reliable for clinical assessment. The child must be taught to breathe in fully to total lung capacity and then to blow out as far and as fast as he can until residual volume is reached. The volume can then be measured manually or calculated automatically with the help of a simple microprocessor.

The advantage of this technique is that the measurement is more reproducible than the PEFR and is rather less dependent on the child's maximal efforts. The disadvantage is that more co-ordination is required, young children tending not to blow out to residual volume before commencing their next breath. A further problem is that young children tend to have a faster time constant than adults so that the FEV_1 approaches or even equals the vital capacity. This reduces the sensitivity of the test as the measurement is then on the flat and relatively insensitive part of the curve (see Figure 3.4). One way to overcome this is to measure the volume expressed in 0.75 s ($FEV_{0.75}$) rather than the traditional 1 s.[2]

The FEV may also be expressed as a percentage of the vital capacity. For the reasons

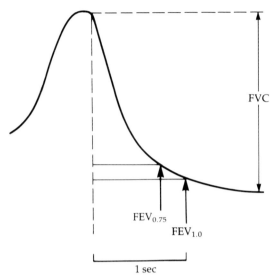

Figure 3.4 In young children the FEV$_1$ closely
approaches the forced vital capacity. The FEV$_{0.75}$
provides a more sensitive index of airways obstruction.

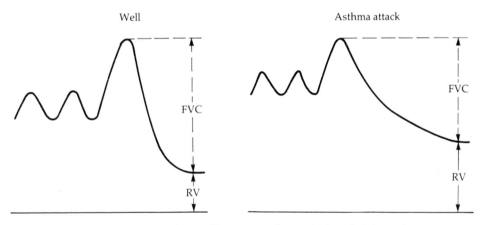

Figure 3.5 In asthma the residual volume will increase, reducing the forced vital capacity.

stated above, it is then preferable to use the FEV$_{0.75}$ which approximates to the FEV$_1$/VC ratio used in adult practice (ie, a value below 70 per cent suggests some degree of airways obstruction). The main attractions of this are firstly that reference to normal data is avoided, and secondly that healthy children with low normal vital capacity results, who will then inevitably also have reduced FEV results, will not be considered abnormal. The disadvantage is that as small-airways obstruction progresses and the residual volume increases, the vital capacity will itself be reduced. Inevitably the FEV$_1$/VC ratio will then tend to underestimate the amount of airways obstruction (see Figure 3.5).

Sometimes the FEV trace is used to derive the mean flow across the mid-portion of the curve, the maximum mid-expiratory flow (MMEF$_{25-75}$). This is obtained by drawing a

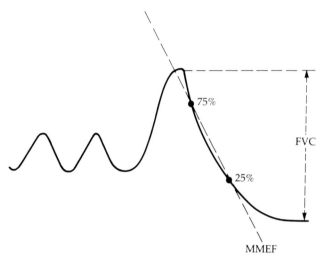

Figure 3.6 The maximum mid-expiratory flow is derived from the slope of the line which runs through points 25 and 75 per cent up the forced vital capacity curve.

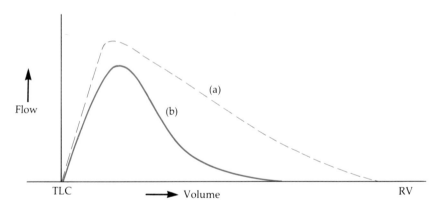

Figure 3.7 The flow volume curves from a child when well (a) and during an asthma attack (b).

line between the 25 per cent and 75 per cent volume points (see Figure 3.6). This is found to be a more sensitive index of airways obstruction but is also less reproducible (coefficient of variation approximately 20 per cent).[3] It has therefore little advantage to offer over the standard FEV measurement.

Flow volume curves

Further information can be derived by plotting the expired flow against the volume trace. The flow can be obtained from the spirometer using a differentiator. Alternatively, the flow signal from a pneumotachograph can be plotted against the integrated volume result. A typical pattern is shown in Figure 3.7. In the normal child, the trace from the point of maximum flow to residual volume (RV) will be convex. If airways obstruction is present, the trace will become concave so that deviations from normal will be greatest at relatively low lung volumes. The measurements usually defined from the trace are the PEFR and flows at 25 per cent, 50 per cent and 75 per cent of lung volume, forced expiratory flow (FEF)$_{25, 50, or 75}$. Of these the most useful is the FEF$_{75}$, as this is less dependent on the child's expiratory effort (ie, increasing efforts will not increase the flow once the flow limit has been reached). This volume also provides useful information on the small airways as at this part of expiration the flow rate is largely limited by the small airways.[4]

The main disadvantage of this measurement is that comparison between breaths is difficult if the child produces different vital capacities. One way round this is to assume that the child starts at the same point at the beginning of expiration (ie, that the total lung capacity (TLC) remains relatively constant). If one curve is then plotted on top of another, the FEF$_{75}$ of the greatest curve can then be used as the reference point.

Partial flow volume curves

Some authorities claim that the partial flow volume curve provides more sensitive information on changes in airways obstruction. For this the child blows forcibly out from the top of a normal tidal breath using a device for measuring both flow and volume. He then breathes in immediately to total lung capacity and blows out again to residual volume. The second trace is used to define the FEF$_{75}$ point but the flow rate is read from the initial curve.

The advantage of this technique is that the full inspiration may induce a degree of bronchodilatation and so hide early bronchoconstrictor responses to histamine or other challenges. Conversely, the inspiratory effort sometimes leads to bronchoconstriction. Although there is evidence to suggest that this technique is useful in adults, such information as is available on children does not suggest that it is a major advance.[6]

Plethysmography

Total body plethysmography provides the possibility not only of measuring the total volume of air in the lungs[7] and hence the degree of hyperinflation, but also of measuring the airways resistance directly.[5] The technique assumes that when the child pants against a closed shutter system while situated in an airtight container (the plethysmograph), the pressure changes recorded at the child's mouth are identical to those in the alveoli (see Figure 3.8). The thoracic volume changes responsible for the pressure swings are measured as pressure changes within the plethysmograph. These can be converted to volume changes by calibration against a syringe. From the changes in alveolar volume and the corresponding changes in intrathoracic pressure, the volume of air in the lungs at the point at which the shutter was closed can be calculated using Boyle's law:

$$P_1V_1 = P_2V_2$$

where P_1 represents the atmospheric pressure (P atmos) and V_1 represents the volume air in the lungs (thoracic gas volume, or TGV). To a close approximation this can be expressed as follows:

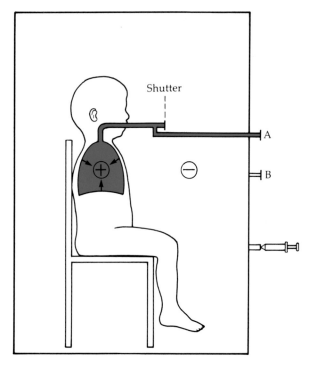

Figure 3.8 The measurement of thoracic gas volume.
The child is breathing out against a closed shutter.
This produces a fall in pressure within the plethysmograph.

$$\text{TGV} = \frac{\Delta V}{\Delta P} \times P_{atmos}$$

where ΔV and ΔP represent changes in intrathoracic volume and pressure during breathing movements against a closed shutter.

By measuring tidal volume before shutter closure and encouraging the child to breathe in fully and then blow out maximally, it is possible to measure both the total lung capacity and the residual volume as well as the thoracic gas volume (see Figure 3.9). In an asthma attack first the residual volume and then the thoracic gas volume will be increased, often by as much as 200 per cent. The total lung capacity may also be increased, but by a smaller proportion. It has recently been shown that if there is severe airways obstruction with extensive air trapping, the mouth pressure may underestimate the mean alveolar pressure. Under these circumstances the thoracic gas volume will be overestimated. This can be avoided by closing the shutter at the top rather than at the bottom of the tidal breath and then subtracting the tidal volume.[6]

Airways resistance   Total body plethysmograph pressure swings are also seen as the child breathes or pants through the shutter/pneumotachograph system, even though there is no change in total air volume, merely a transfer of gas between the lungs and the volume within the body plethysmograph. This is due to changes in alveolar pressure which are generated by the respiratory muscles to pull and push air in and out of the

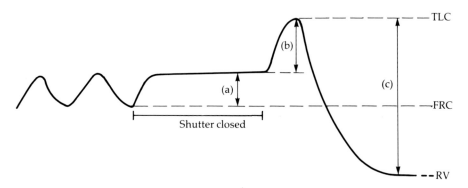

Figure 3.9 Volume trace during plethysmography. The TGV is measured at the top of the normal breath. The FRC is calculated by subtracting (a), the TLC by adding (b), and the RV by subtracting (c) from the TLC.

lungs. Once the thoracic gas volume is measured using the techniques described above, the pressure changes in the alveoli can be calculated by converting the pressure changes within the total body plethysmograph to volume changes and substituting the values in the following formula which is again based on Boyle's Law:

$$P_A = \frac{\Delta V}{TGV} \times P_{atmos}$$

where P_A is the alveolar pressure and ΔV is the intrathoracic volume change due to air compression in inspiration.

Once the alveolar pressure changes are known, the airways resistance (R_{aw}) can be calculated:[7]

$$R_{aw} = \frac{\Delta P_A}{\Delta \overset{\circ}{V}}$$

where $\Delta \overset{\circ}{V}$ is the flow rate at the mouth.

Resistance is not constant throughout the tidal breath, however, when airways obstruction is present. This is due to turbulence at high flow rates and dynamic compression on expiration. As a result it is customary to measure the resistance at flow rates of either 0.5 or 1.0 l/s during inspiration. Over these ranges air flow will be laminar.

Because airways resistance tends to fall as lung volume increases, the results of body plethysmography are sometimes expressed as specific conductance:

$$1 \cdot R_{aw} \cdot TGV$$

One major advantage is that this measurement is virtually constant throughout life, with normal values of 0.15–0.30. As airways obstruction increases, the specific conductance will tend to fall.

The main advantages of the plethysmograph measurements are that they are independent of the child's efforts, and provide direct information on airways calibre and the extent of lung hyperinflation.[8] The main disadvantage is that these techniques are not easy for young children (less than seven years old). Some children find the chambers claustrophobic, and the cost of equipment is high.

Gas dilution technique

Sometimes the functional residual capacity (FRC), TLC and RV are measured using closed-circuit gas dilution techniques.[9] For this the child breathes in and out of a circuit comprising a spirometer, a circulating pump and a carbon dioxide absorber. The volume of the circuit and the concentration of a tracer gas, usually helium, can be measured. The child breathes in and out of the circuit for 4 min while oxygen is bled into the circuit to compensate for the carbon dioxide which is absorbed. The volume of air in the child's lung at the point of connection can be calculated by substitution in the following formula:

$$FRC = \frac{C_1 - C_2}{C_2} \times V_S$$

where C_1 and C_2 are the initial and final concentrations of the tracer gas and V_S is the volume of gas in the circuit before the child is connected.

At the end of the 4 min of rebreathing, the child can be encouraged to take a deep breath in and then perform a forced expiratory vital capacity manoeuvre so that TLC and RV can also be calculated.

The advantages of this technique are that the equipment is relatively cheap, and the results reproducible. The disadvantage is that as airways obstruction increases, the tracer gas is unlikely to be freely distributed throughout the lung because of gas trapping, so that the true lung volume will tend to be underestimated.

It is also possible to measure the lung volume using an open-circuit system whereby the child breathes through a one-way valve system.[10] The inspiratory gas is changed to 100 per cent oxygen at the end of the quiet expiration. The nitrogen content of the expired gas is monitored until this is less than 2 per cent. All the expired gases are collected. By measuring the volume and the nitrogen content of the expired gas, the volume of nitrogen washed out of the lungs can be calculated. By knowing the initial and final nitrogen concentration in the lungs, the volume of gas in the lungs at the time of connection can be estimated. The advantages of this technique are that the apparatus is relatively cheap, and analysis of the nitrogen washout curve can provide additional information on air trapping. The disadvantage is that if there is severe airways obstruction with air trapping, full clearance of nitrogen will not be achieved and the lung volume will again be underestimated. Conversely, nitrogen will be washed out of body tissues and this will tend to have the reverse effect on results.

CHILDREN AGED THREE TO FIVE YEARS

Children between the age of three and five years present a far greater challenge. Few under the age of five are able to blow out to RV sufficiently well to make spirometry a practical proposition, and as a result no normal data are available. Standard plethysmography is also out of the question. Most, however, are happy to blow into peak flow meters,[11] preferably using devices which record over the 20–200 l/min range. Results are less reproducible than in older children but nevertheless, after appropriate training, peak flow measurements can be used to establish a diagnosis and to monitor progress.

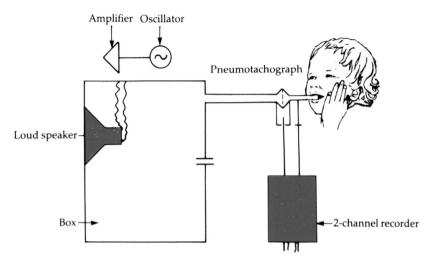

Figure 3.10 Forced oscillation system.

Forced oscillation technique

One technique which has proved useful is the forced oscillation technique. In health, the respiratory system—like an organ pipe, empty bottle or suspension bridge—has a natural resonance frequency. If the respiratory system is stimulated or driven at this frequency, the only limiting factor to the oscillation is the resistance of the airways, lung tissues and chest wall. The two other normally opposing mechanical factors, the compliance and the inertia are by definition equal at the resonance frequency and as they are 180° out of phase, they will cancel each other out. This frequency is virtually constant at 4–10 cycles/s throughout life. This phenomenon is well recognized by dogs, who elect to pant at their resonance frequency as this allows them to exchange large quantities of air and thus lose heat with the minimum of effort!

The standard technique is to generate a sine wave pressure change within a box using a loudspeaker, audio amplifier and sine wave generator. The pressure changes are conducted down a wide-bore tube to a flow-measuring device, a pneumotachograph, and beyond that a mouthpiece (see Figure 3.10). All that is required is for the child to breathe quietly in and out of the system while his cheeks are supported. It is then possible to measure the resistance of the respiratory system simply by dividing the pressure oscillations at the mouth by the flow oscillations.[12]

The advantage of this technique is that the results are independent of the child's efforts and make few demands on the child's cooperation. The disadvantage is that if the child breathes out too quickly or closes his glottis, the measurements will be affected as they are very sensitive to changes in upper airways calibre. Nevertheless, the coefficient of variation for this measurement is usually less than 10 per cent. Additional information can be obtained if a range of frequencies are used or if numerous frequencies (white noise) are generated at the same time. Both of these approaches need sophisticated computing systems and are not suitable at the moment for routine clinical practice.

Functional residual capacity

Some authors[13] have managed to obtain information on lung volumes using a suitably designed closed-circuit gas dilution technique and face mask rather than a mouth tube.

THE FIRST THREE YEARS

Lung function measurements in younger children present even greater problems. The only exception to this is the neonatal period, as newborn babies are sufficiently sleepy and acquiescent to tolerate face masks without the need for sedation. Information in the first three years of life has, however, been obtained using several different approaches.

Forced oscillation technique

The forced oscillation technique described earlier (see page 27) can be used, substituting a face mask for the mouthpiece.[14] As with all other measurements in infancy, results will be influenced by nasal obstruction which is unfortunately a common finding in wheezy children. Pretreatment with vasoconstrictor agents, such as xylometazoline (0.05 per cent), helps overcome this.

Total body plethysmography

It is also possible to collect information on lung volumes and airways resistance using specially constructed total body plethysmographs in which sedated infants can be studied, either lying supine or preferably in the lateral position. Thoracic gas volume measurements present little difficulty.[15] For airways resistance measurements, it is necessary either to heat the gas within the total body plethysmograph to 37°C/98°F and ensure a high degree of humidification or to arrange for the baby to rebreathe from a heated humidified anaesthetic rebreathing bag lying within the body of the plethysmograph.[16] If these precautions are not taken, large errors will be introduced due to the heating and cooling of air as it is transferred in and out of the baby's lungs.

Total pulmonary resistance

It is possible to record the intrathoracic respiratory pressure swings by measuring pressure changes in the lower third of the oesophagus. Micropressure transducers are available which can be mounted on standard feeding tubes and passed either through the mouth or via the nares. Alternatively the pressures can be recorded from fluid-filled and perfused catheters which open in the lower third of the oesophagus. Some workers prefer to use thin-walled balloons mounted on the end of feeding catheters (see Figure 3.11). If the flow and volume changes are recorded simultaneously by a pneumotachograph and integrator system, the total pulmonary resistance can be measured by identifying points of equal volume on inspiration and expiration (ie, points at which the elastic recoil will be equal). If the differences in pressure are divided by the differences in flow between these two points, the total pulmonary resistance will be measured (see Figure 3.12).

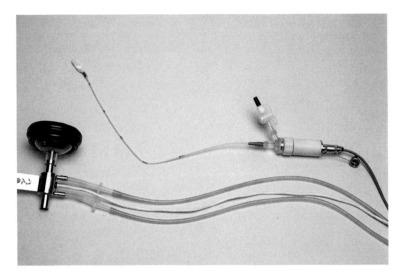

Figure 3.11 Oesophageal balloon.

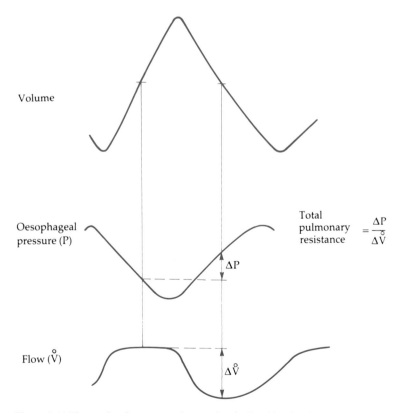

Figure 3.12 The total pulmonary resistance is calculated by dividing the pressure difference at the mid-volume points by the simultaneous flow differences.

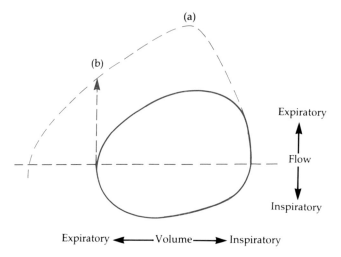

Figure 3.13 A typical forced partial expiratory flow volume curve from a normal infant. Data are collected at peak flow (a) and FRC (b).

Partial expiratory flow volume curves

It has recently become possible to obtain information on the airways of sedated infants in the first year of life by engulfing their chests and volumes in inflatable jackets which have relatively rigid outer walls.[17] The jackets are rapidly inflated to pressures of 30–40 cmH$_2$O at the very beginning of expiration using a compressed air reservoir. The resulting expiratory flow volume curve is recorded by a pneumotachograph and integrator system.

The advantages of this system are that the equipment is relatively cheap, and the results seen reproducible. The disadvantage is that the squeeze stimulates the baby to make inspiratory efforts which will tend to modify the expiratory flow volume curve.[18] Normal data are limited, but it is now possible to collect information both on the peak flow generated and the flow at the normal end-expiratory point (FRC) as determined by previous breaths (see Figure 3.13).

PRACTICAL POINTS

- Lung function tests provide useful objective information on the degree of airways obstruction.

- These tests have an important part to play in diagnosis and in assessing the response to therapy. They are invaluable in research investigations.

- For clinical use, frequent simple measurements, for example, peak flow, are preferable to occasional and more sophisticated methods of investigation.

4
Diagnosis

DANGER OF UNDERDIAGNOSIS

Childhood asthma is still grossly underdiagnosed, perhaps more so than any other condition in childhood. Some doctors tend to equate asthma solely with wheezing brought on by an allergic trigger. Many prefer to use labels such as 'wheezy bronchitis', particularly if viral infections are the predominant aetiological factor, on the assumption that the label of 'asthma' will generate too much anxiety in the parents. Epidemiological studies have failed to support this concept, showing rather that, provided a correct diagnosis leads to appropriate therapy, anxiety is greatly relieved rather than increased.[1] **In practice, the diagnosis of asthma should be made on all children who have symptoms arising from abnormal airways lability sufficient to prevent them from leading a normal life.**

The diagnosis is largely based on the history. Although there are many causes of wheezing in childhood, particularly in early infancy, in at least 90 per cent of cases the underlying problems will be that of asthma (see Table 4.1). Not all asthmatic children have episodes of breathlessness. The large majority will have coughing, particularly at night, often causing other members of the family to waken from their sleep. From the practical point of view, all children with recurrent attacks of coughing and wheezing should be considered asthmatic until proved otherwise. Some asthmatic children, particularly those under the age of five years, will have bouts of coughing at night and often further attacks on exercise without obvious breathlessness or wheezing. Although these children have a relatively mild form of asthma, they are well worth identifying as response to appropriate management is almost always dramatic—unlike all other causes of recurrent or persistent coughing in childhood (see Table 4.2).

Children who have normal airways lability as a secondary phenomenon provide a greater classification problem. It is well recognized that children with cystic fibrosis will be more likely to have a degree of reversible airways obstruction than will a normal control population.[2] This appears to be due to true abnormal lability rather than normal lability superimposed on reduced airways calibre. A similar pattern is often seen in bronchiectasis due to other causes including the immotile cilia syndrome, and in children who have inhaled foreign bodies or even experienced a drowning episode.[3] Although these children have symptoms due to their abnormal airways lability and respond well to bronchodilator drugs, the natural history is obviously determined by the underlying cause and so tends to be different from that of a primary asthmatic problem.

Table 4.1 Causes of wheezing in childhood

Asthma
Bronchiolitis
Cystic fibrosis
Aspiration
Milk
Foreign body
Irreversible airways obstruction
Bronchomalacia
Tracheal/bronchial stenosis
Vascular rings
Mediastinal tumours

Table 4.2 Causes of coughing in childhood

Asthma
Bronchitis
Whooping cough
Bronchiolitis
Bronchiectasis
Cystic fibrosis
Aspiration
Milk
Foreign body
Mediastinal tumours
Laryngeal/tracheal stenosis
Psychogenic

INITIAL ASSESSMENT WHEN ASTHMA IS SUSPECTED

History

It is necessary to get a clear picture of the severity of the child's symptoms, the impact these symptoms are having on the child and his family, and information on trigger factors. This information is likely to be of considerably more value to the management strategy than all subsequent investigations. Points which need to be sought include:

- Age at onset
- Nature of symptoms
- Triggers
  - —Are all the attacks produced by upper respiratory tract infections?
  - —Does contact with animals, pollens, or food items have any influence on symptoms?
  - —Is EIB present all the time or only intermittently?
- Severity of symptoms
  - —Are these relatively trivial to the child and causing anxiety only to the parents?
  - —Has the child ever had to be admitted to hospital?
  - —Does he ever get acutely breathless or even cyanosed?
- Pattern of attacks
  - —Does the child have only occasional attacks, with long periods when he is asymptomatic? If so, how long do the attacks last? If the symptoms are present virtually all the time, does the severity alter much?
  - —Are the symptoms worse at any particular time of the day or during one particular season?
- Impact
  - —Is the child usually able to go to school/playschool during attacks?
  - —How much school attendance is missed?
  - —Is the child able to take part fully in physical activities at school and at home?

- Therapy
    —What drugs has the child required so far?
    —How effective have these drugs been?
    —When do the parents consider these drugs should be given?
    —What other measures have been taken to modify the cause, eg, house dust avoidance?

Family details

It is also well worth enquiring whether asthma or atopy of any kind affects first- or second-degree relatives. If asthma is present in the family more information should be obtained on its severity, as this is likely to influence the parents'—and perhaps the child's—concept of asthma, particularly if the condition has responded poorly to treatment or has even been responsible for a death.

Past illnesses

Document previous illness. As described elsewhere (see page 94), asthma symptoms are extremely common after attacks of acute bronchiolitis[4] and also after *Mycoplasma pneumoniae*[5] and other lung insults, including bronchial foreign bodies. Some parents date the onset of symptoms to an attack of measles or whooping cough, but there is currently no evidence to suggest that either of these conditions produces longterm lung abnormalities.[6]

Obstetric and birth history

There are now two reports indicating that the incidence of asthma is increased in babies born prematurely. It is also likely that babies who have required intensive ventilator therapy in the neonatal period are more likely to have abnormal airways lability at least for the next one to two years.

Clinical assessment

Growth   There will be no growth retardation due to asthma unless the child has severe and virtually continuous symptoms with chest deformity. The weight centile is then likely to be lower than that for height (see Figure 4.1a,b). There is no evidence to suggest that this is due to a failure of growth hormone secretions. Growth delay can obviously also be caused by systemic steroids, although it is unlikely to occur unless the dose exceeds $5\,mg/m^2$ surface area per day and is maintained for many months.[11] Growth suppression has not been recorded as a complication of topical steroids.

Clubbing   It is standard medical teaching that asthma does not cause clubbing. However, there are some asthmatic children who have clinically apparent changes. These may be familial in origin, but can also be due to bronchiectasis. As already stated, bronchiectasis may produce a degree of abnormal airways lability—presumably representing a non-specific reaction to airways inflammation. It is worth remembering that bronchiectasis can also be secondary to lobar collapse arising from bronchial plugging. This collapse usually resolves spontaneously, but may persist with secondary infection leading to bronchiectasis.

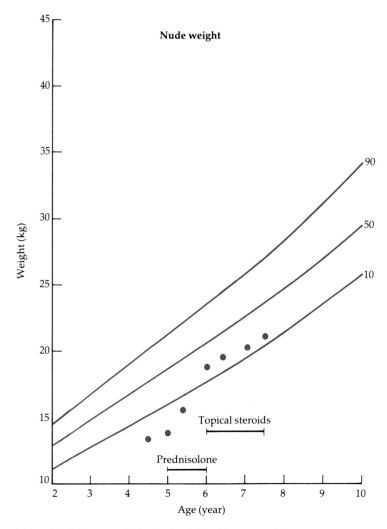

Figure 4.1a,b The growth charts of a child with severe asthma.
Initially, the child's weight is at a lower centile than his height. This
is reversed during a year of oral steroids. Growth improves once he
is changed on to inhaled topical steroids.

Cyanosis Desaturation occurs early in asthma due to abnormalities in ventilation/
perfusion distribution (see page 95), and some children with extensive small-airways
involvement and hyperinflation may have a clinically detectable degree of cyanosis even
when not breathless or wheezy.

Chest deformity with bilateral Harrison sulci, increased anterior and posterior diameter,
and prominence of the upper chest indicates that the child has had frequent or chronic
airways obstruction. The deformity occurs most frequently in young children who have
relatively malleable chest walls (see Figure 4.2). These signs are well worth looking for,
as they often provide more information on the severity of the child's asthma than is
apparent from the parents' story. Reduced cardiac dullness is a difficult sign to identify

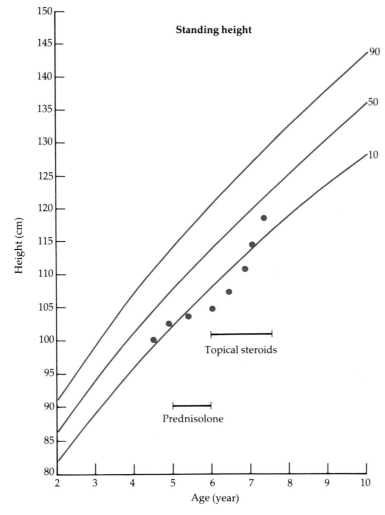

Figure 4.1b

but, when present, provides additional information on the degree of hyperinflation. It is also worth documenting the displacement of the liver edge down into the abdomen, again as an index of hyperinflation.

Auscultation is a useful procedure, as rhonchi are often present at times when the child is not obviously wheezy. It also helps to identify those children, referred to as 'chesty', who have coarse crackling sounds due to excessive upper airways secretions. This often occurs in children who have cerebral palsy or other neuromuscular problems, but is also found in otherwise healthy young infants and is not particularly associated with asthma. The rhonchi are often inspiratory as well as expiratory and may be associated with coarse crepitations. Fine crepitations (ie, sounds arising from the small airways or alveoli) strongly suggest that the underlying condition is not asthma but some structural

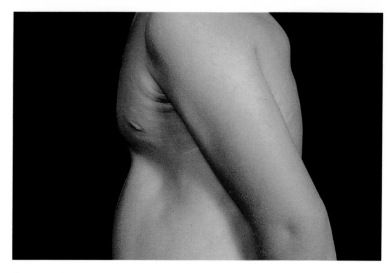

Figure 4.2 Severe chest deformity in a young child with asthma.

damage, for example, obliterative bronchiolitis or even fibrosing alveolitis. The amplitude of the rhonchi correlates poorly with the degree of airways obstruction. The reason for this is that the rhonchi are generated by turbulent flow in the larger airways and trachea. If the child has severe small-airways obstruction he may be unable to generate sufficient flow to create turbulence. These children may only start to have obvious wheezing when given a bronchodilator drug.

INITIAL INVESTIGATIONS

Lung function tests

Simple lung function tests are an essential part of the management of asthma. For routine outpatient or surgery assessment, regular measurements with simple peak flow recording devices are far preferable to occasional but more sophisticated measurements of lung function. Any of the devices currently available for measuring peak flow are adequate for this purpose (see Figure 3.2 on page 19). A peak flow meter can, in the first instance, provide diagnostic information. Improvement of more than 15 per cent after an inhaled beta$_2$ stimulant from an aerosol, a powder delivery system or a nebulizer confirms that the child has abnormal airways lability. If the history is suggestive and the improvement is less than 15 per cent, check the baseline peak flow against that expected for height (see Figure 4.3). It may be that the child is particularly well at the time and is already maximally bronchodilated. If so, check the child on another day, preferably when he has symptoms. It is rarely necessary to proceed to bronchoconstrictor challenges, such as histamine or exercise, in the clinical situation. The peak flow is also essential for follow-up assessments, providing a measurement which is independent of the doctor's evaluation and the parents' impression of the severity of the child's

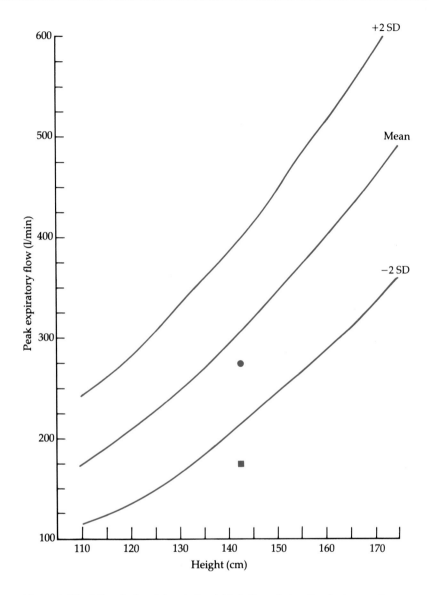

Figure 4.3 Peak flow before (■) and after (●) inhaling a beta$_2$ stimulant aerosol.

symptoms. This is important, as some parents—and indeed some children—greatly underestimate the severity of the asthma, while others tend to concentrate all the family's anxieties on the child's asthma although this may in fact be relatively mild. It may be helpful to provide the family with a diary card and peak flow meter, so that symptoms and lung function and drug usage can be recorded on a 12-hourly basis. It is, however, necessary to stress that the correlation between either the clinician's or the patient's assessment of asthma severity and peak flow or FEV measurements is relatively poor. Referral for more sophisticated lung function tests is indicated only if the child has severe asthma which does not seem to be responding to treatment. It is then important to see whether this is due simply to the fact that the child is receiving inadequate therapy, or whether there is a degree of irreversible airways obstruction with underlying structural lung damage. Lung function tests (spirometry, flow volume curves and plethysmography) before and after two weeks of systemic steroid therapy (eg, prednisolone 1–2 mg/kg per day) will usually resolve this problem (see Figure 4.4).

Full blood picture

Few children referred for assessment escape this investigation, although the results rarely (if ever) have any impact on management. Even those with severe chronic symptoms do not develop polycythaemia, and the eosinophil count is not always elevated (greater than $500/mm^3$). If a high level is found it is rarely possible to identify where this indicates that there is a strong allergic basis to the asthma. These children often have associated eczema. In addition, eosinophilia is not an uncommon finding in otherwise entirely healthy children (see Table 4.3).

Table 4.3 Causes of eosinophilia in childhood
Asthma ⎫ *commonest*   Eczema ⎭
Bronchopulmonary aspergillosis   Dermatitis herpetiformis   Eosinophilia leukaemia   Worm infestation   Addison's disease   Tropical eosinophilia

Table 4.4 Commonly used antigens for skin tests
Negative control (diluent)   Positive control (histamine)   House dust   *D. pteronyssinus*   Cat   Dog   Feathers   Grass pollens   Tree pollens   Moulds

Immunoglobulin levels

Blood is frequently sent off to be tested for immunoglobulin levels. Typically the IgG and IgA levels will be normal in childhood asthma. Some young children have low IgA levels in association with relatively troublesome symptoms. It is claimed by some that an improvement is seen as the IgA level recovers later in childhood.[7] Total IgE levels are almost always increased in children with asthma. Often this merely provides information which is supportive to the history, rather than providing new light on the child's status. It is now possible to measure plasma IgE which is specific to a variety of potential allergens using radioimmunoassay techniques—the RAST test. These tests are relatively expensive and, although correlating reasonably well with skin tests, correlate less well with bronchial challenge tests than information derived from a careful history. Such tests are rarely helpful in the situation where they would be most useful, that is, identifying important food allergens.

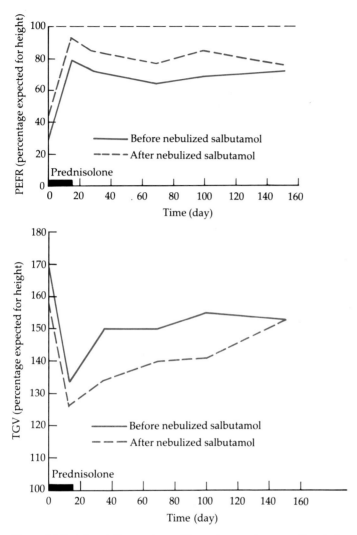

Figure 4.4 Serial peak flow meter and thoracic gas volume readings in ten children with severe asthma. A two week course of prednisolone dramatically improved peak flow before and after nebulized salbutamol.

Skin tests (see Figure 4.5a–d)

These are often requested by parents in the hope that they will lead to the identification of the cause of their child's asthma. They are relatively reproducible (see Table 4.4), painless and easy to carry out.

The standard techniques are either to scratch the surface of the skin through a droplet of solution containing a possible antigen or, perhaps more satisfactorily, to press the tip of the needle against the skin at 30° to the surface; as the skin is depressed so the tip

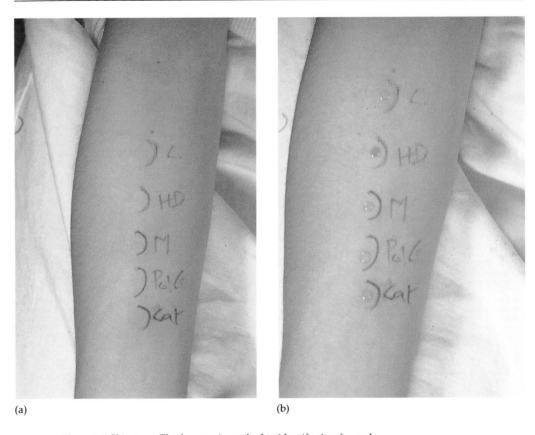

(a)   (b)

Figure 4.5 Skin tests. The forearm is marked to identify sites for each allergen (a). Drops of allergen solution are placed on the skin (b). The point of a disposable needle held almost parallel to the skin is depressed, introducing the solution to the superficial layers of the epidermis (c). A new needle is used for each solution. The diameter of urticaria (not erythema) is measured (d) — 2 mm or more represents a positive response.

penetrates the outer layers of the epidermis. It is essential to include a negative control (ie, the carrier solution), and preferably to have a positive control as well—1:1000 histamine. It is usual to test against a minimum of house dust, house dust mite, cat, and grass pollens, but the possibilities are virtually endless and selection can best be made by referring to the history. A positive result is usually defined as a weal which is greater than 2 mm in diameter after 20 min. Once the results have been documented, it is usual to apply a mild local anaesthetic cream to the skin to eliminate the itching sensation. The large majority of child asthmatics will have several positive reactions, with a tendency for the number of positive reactions to increase with age. Unfortunately approximately 50 per cent of non-asthmatic children will also have at least one positive reaction. Some children will have only one or two strongly positive reactions, indicating that the child is particularly sensitive to these allergens, but, as with specific IgE results, this information will almost always be available from the history. For example, a child who has a strong skin reaction to cat fur will often have a history of developing facial oedema,

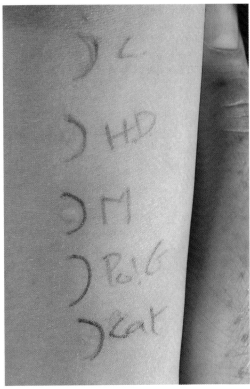

(c) (d)

conjunctivitis, coughing and wheezing after brief contact with a cat. Like the IgE results, the skin reaction to food allergens correlates very poorly with their clinical relevance and is generally accepted as unhelpful or even possibly misleading in clinical practice.[9] Approximately 50 per cent of all children have positive reactions to cow's milk protein.

The relationship between positive skin tests and positive bronchial provocation tests is also poor. This relationship improves when the skin test is particularly positive.

Conjunctival provocation

Some authorities recommend conjunctival provocation,[10] placing droplets of weak allergen solutions into the inner corner of the eye. A positive reaction produces itching, watering and sometimes hyperaemia of the conjunctiva. Again the correlation between positive conjunctival and bronchial provocation test is far from perfect, and this technique is less readily accepted by the child.

Nasal provocation

The nasal mucosa has been similarly explored, using itching and sneezing as a positive response.[10] This has proved a useful tool in the investigation of allergic rhinitis, but has the same poor correlation with clinical asthma.

Bronchial provocation

It is relatively easy to induce and measure the bronchoconstrictor response to a variety of stimuli including exercise, histamine, methacholine, cold air and ultrasonically nebulized distilled water (see page 12). These provide an index of the degree of airways lability and have been used with great success to define different epidemiological groups. There is general agreement that those with most symptoms tend to have most airways lability. At the individual level the tests are less helpful, because for those with mild, ill-defined symptoms where a positive diagnosis is most needed, the response often falls within the normal range.[10] There are also a considerable number of children who are asymptomatic and who have a measure of abnormal airways lability.[11] For these reasons bronchial challenges are rarely required in clinical practice.

Allergen bronchial provocation

This provides a tool for evaluating the response to allergens under control conditions. The technique is time consuming, however, and only one allergen can be tested at a time. As late reactions sometimes occur, most authorities consider that children under investigation should be kept in hospital under observation for the night after the study. Others give systemic steroids, 10–20 mg prednisolone as a single dose, in the knowledge that this is safe and will not influence the immediate reaction but will block any late reaction. These problems limit such investigations to research laboratories.

PRACTICAL POINTS

- Childhood asthma is still grossly underdiagnosed.

- The diagnosis assessment depends largely on a careful history; all children with wheezing attacks should be regarded as asthmatic until proven otherwise.

- The degree of chest deformity can give useful information on the severity of symptoms in the past.

- Simple and frequent lung function tests are essential in assessment and management, providing independent and objective measurements of airflow obstruction.

- Full blood pictures, and total and specific IgE are rarely helpful in management. Skin tests rarely modify treatment.

- Bronchial provocation tests should be limited to research investigations.

These
shou...

Use them as a bas...
with tutors and in pa...
discussions with the 4
students.

5
Drug treatment

ASSESSMENT OF SEVERITY

The advice and information given to the family, indeed the therapy selected, will depend to a large degree on the severity of the asthma. Asthma represents a continuous spectrum, from relatively trivial symptoms of coughing and wheezing once or twice a year to chronic asthma with growth retardation, chest deformity and such severe symptoms that the child affected is virtually a respiratory cripple. Fortunately the pattern of asthma follows one limb of what is an almost normal distribution curve, which means that the percentage of children affected is inversely related to the severity of their condition. From the practical point of view it is useful to categorize the children into groups based loosely on those devised by the Melbourne group.[1] This categorization is based on symptom frequency and severity, and as it formed the basis of a longterm follow-up it provides parents with information on the likely longterm outcome. The groups are as follows:

- Children with occasional attacks of coughing and wheezing, usually brought on by viral respiratory tract infections and with relatively long intervening asymptomatic periods
- Children with frequent but not particularly severe attacks of asthma but again with intervening periods when they are entirely well
- Children whose asthma is again episodic but in whom the attacks can be very severe, sometimes requiring admission to hospital or oral steroid therapy
- Children with chronic symptoms, often with acute exacerbations.

Once the diagnosis of asthma has been reached, time must be set aside to make certain that the parents and, where appropriate, the child (particularly if over the age of eight years) understand what is meant by the diagnosis and how its impact on the child and on family life can be limited. It is essential that the parents are provided with information on the differences between bronchodilator and prophylactic therapy. They need to know what to do in an acute attack and to be able to identify when the asthma is severe and no longer responding adequately to therapy, that is, the times when it is imperative that they seek extra help either from their family doctor or a local hospital. They will also seek information on the short-term and longterm outcome, whether their

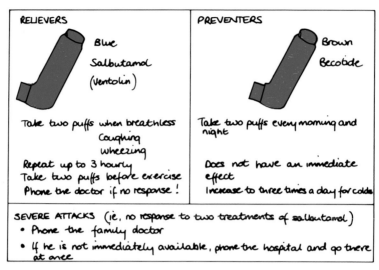

RELIEVERS

Blue
Salbutamol
(Ventolin)

Take two puffs when breathless
Coughing
wheezing
Repeat up to 3 hourly
Take two puffs before exercise
Phone the doctor if no response!

PREVENTERS

Brown
Becotide

Take two puffs every morning and night

Does not have an immediate effect
Increase to three times a day for colds

SEVERE ATTACKS (ie, no response to two treatments of salbutamol)
• Phone the family doctor
• If he is not immediately available, phone the hospital and go there at once

Figure 5.1 A completed patient education card for an asthmatic child.

child should take part in all school activities, and when it is reasonable for the child to stay at home.

It is essential to appreciate that after such an interview the parents are unlikely to have taken in and remembered more than 20 per cent of the information that has been imparted, even though the physician considers him- or herself to be a highly skilled communicator. For this reason, the parents of the child should be given other information sources that they can go over later to reinforce what they have been told once they have returned home. We do not yet know the most effective means for this education process. It is certain that a variety of approaches are needed so that the family can then select the presentation which suits them best. Some physicians, particularly those with artistic skills, construct simple charts with illustrations and minimal wording while discussing the various aspects with the parents and the child. The chart is then given to the family and can be used as an aide-memoire (see Figure 5.1). There are now a number of booklets and comics available that can be issued at the end of the appointment. It is also well worth giving parents the telephone number of the local asthma group which, in the UK, will have access to information pamphlets issued by the National Asthma Society. Many people find that spoken information is easier to retain. For this reason, tapes have been produced that can be loaned or given to families. Most find that listening to tapes on several occasions will considerably increase their knowledge and confidence so that they can cope with day-to-day problems and also the occasional acute severe attack (see Appendix page 130).

Drug therapy

As there are a number of particular problems in the delivery and selection of drugs in young children, three age groups will be considered separately—children over the age of five years, those between the ages of one and five years, and those in the first year of life. These age groups are to some extent arbitrary and there will inevitably be a considerable degree of overlap, depending on the child's development.

Drugs used in the treatment of asthma are usually separated into those which produce relief within minutes (bronchodilator drugs) and those which are prophylactic, reducing the frequency and severity of attacks. All children with asthma of sufficient severity to require treatment will need bronchodilator drugs. The minimal indications for prophylactic therapy remain poorly defined and certainly differ from one part of the world to another and from one unit to another. There is a hypothesis that the generous introduction of prophylactic drugs may improve the longterm outcome, but the information in support of this is very limited. It is known that a late reaction to an antigen challenge will increase abnormal lability for several weeks.[2] It is not unreasonable to assume that blocking all late reactions, and if possible immediate reactions as well, may reduce the bronchial lability in the long term and perhaps increase the number of children who become symptom free. More work is needed on this area.

CHILDREN OVER THE AGE OF FIVE YEARS

Bronchodilator drugs

It is essential that all children with clinically significant asthma have the ability to relieve acute attacks with an effective bronchodilator drug. There is now no place for the first-generation bronchodilator drugs, adrenaline and isoprenaline. In the past, adrenaline (epinephrine) was given either as a slow subcutaneous injection, as a nebulized solution or as an aerosol (Medihaler). From the therapeutic point of view, the alpha-adrenergic effects might appear to be advantageous, as they reduce mucosal oedema. In practice, although adrenaline is an effective bronchodilator agent, its duration is relatively short and the maximal response is less dramatic than that of the more recent beta$_2$ stimulants.[3] In addition, the relatively strong beta$_1$ adrenergic effects of adrenaline produce unwanted tachycardia and increase cardiac output.

Isoprenaline (isoprel), which can be given as an aerosol or via a nebulizer, has little advantage over adrenaline. It is a non-selected beta stimulant and so will also increase heart rate and cardiac output. It does not, however, have measurable alpha-adrenergic effects. Its duration of action in asthma is virtually the same as that of adrenaline, lasting only 30–60 min. The pharmacological activity of ephedrine is very similar to that of adrenaline, except that it can be taken as either a syrup or tablets. Thus it has both alpha and beta$_1$ and beta$_2$ adrenergic effects. It was used extensively in the treatment of asthma, but in addition to its unwanted cardiac effects it also exhibits tachyphylaxis; a tolerance develops, so that increasing doses are required.

In recent years all these drugs have largely been supplanted by the second-generation beta$_2$ stimulant drugs. There is little to choose between these, although the drug firms have been keen to show differences. Reproterol, for example, has a more rapid onset when inhaled but a shorter duration of action. Terbutaline has a slightly longer than average duration of action. There are, however, no clinical trials to show that any one is superior to the others in domiciliary or hospital practice (see Table 5.1).

Inhalant therapy has many advantages over oral therapy. The onset time is far more rapid—usually 2–5 min compared to 20–30 min (see Figure 5.2). The peak bronchodilator effect also tends to be greater and yet the dose administered is small, often less than 10 per cent of the oral equivalent; this means that side-effects, such as tachycardia and hand tremor, become much less likely. The inhaled route has the additional advantage

Table 5.1 Beta₂ adrenergic stimulant drugs for schoolchildren

Drug (generic name)	Formulation	Dose	Frequency (dose/day)
Fenoterol	Aerosol (180 µg) Respiratory solution (0.5%) (dilute 4–20 times)	1–3 puffs 0.5–1.5 mg	up to 16 up to 6
Pirbuterol	Elixir (7.5 mg/5 ml) Capsule (10 mg) Aerosol (200 µg)	7.5 mg 10 mg 1–3 puffs	up to 4 up to 4 up to 16
Reproterol	Elixir (10 mg/5 ml) Tablets (20 mg) Aerosol (500 µg) Respirator solution (0.1%) (dilute 4 times)	10 mg 10 mg 1–2 puffs 5–10 mg	up to 4 up to 4 up to 16 up to 6
Rimiterol	Aerosol (200 µg) Auto-aerosol (200 µg) Respirator solution (0.5%) (dilute 2 times)	1–3 puffs 1–3 puffs 6.25–12.5 mg	up to 16 up to 16 up to 6
Salbutamol	Elixir (2 mg/5 ml) Tablets (2 mg) Sustained release tablets (8 mg) Aerosol (100 µg) Inhaler powder (200–400 µg) Respirator solution (0.1%) nebules	2–4 mg 2–4 mg 8 mg 1–3 puffs 200–400 µg 2.5–5 mg	up to 4 up to 4 single dose up to 16 up to 6
Terbutaline	Elixir (1.5 mg/5 ml) Tablets (5 mg) Aerosol (250 µg) Aerosol spacer (250 µg) Respirator solution (2.5 mg/ml)	1.5–3 mg 2.5–5 mg 1–3 puffs 1–3 puffs 1.25–2.5 mg	up to 4 up to 4 up to 16 up to 16 up to 6

that it is far more effective in blocking EIB,[4] and indeed it is the treatment of choice for this condition in over 90 per cent of children. The main problem is assuring that the drug is delivered deep into the respiratory tract. The advantage of the oral route is simplicity of administration and a longer duration of action. One laboratory-based study has suggested that optimal bronchodilatation can be achieved by prescribing both oral and inhaled therapy, thereby producing rapid action, maximal peak bronchodilatation and prolonged action (see Figure 5.2).

Selection of devices Of all the delivery devices available, the powder systems (salbutamol Rotacaps, fenoterol, terbutaline) have the most advantages. They are relatively convenient to carry and load and demand a minimum of coordination skills because delivery occurs only as the child breathes in (see Figure 5.3). It is preferable to start all asthmatic children on these devices, even those over the age of eight or nine years who might reasonably be expected to use an aerosol efficiently, so that maximal benefit from beta₂ stimulant therapy can be assessed.

Aerosol therapy can be considered once the child is over the age of seven or eight years and has sufficient maturity to know when to take bronchodilator drugs. Many will still find that the coordination required is beyond them and that powder delivery systems still provide the best measure for relief. The aerosol device is useful only to

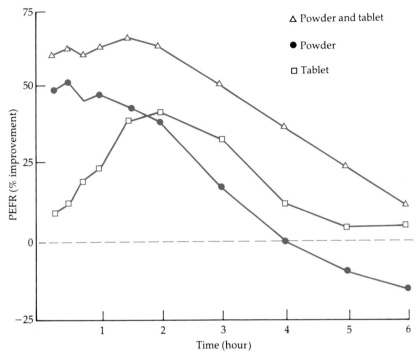

Figure 5.2 Bronchodilator effects of salbutamol powder, tablet and the two combined.

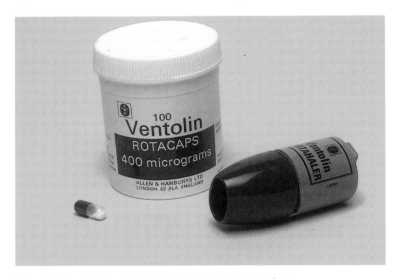

Figure 5.3 A rotahaler device for inhaling drugs as powders.

those who can fire the aerosol soon after the beginning of an inspiration at a point when they are inhaling at a sufficiently high rate to draw the active ingredient down into their lungs; the bulk of the beta$_2$ stimulant is then not impacted on the back of the pharynx. There is some argument about how deeply the child should expire before commencing the inspiration. Most authorities consider that the child should not attempt to reach residual volume, as many of the airways may then be closed when the aerosol is fired. All are agreed that breathing in to full inspiration after firing is an advantage and that if possible the child should then hold his breath for at least 5 s. Radioisotope studies have shown that it is possible to eliminate up to 50 per cent of the inhaled dose by rapid expiration. Using these techniques (see Figure 5.4), up to 10 per cent of the fired dose is likely to reach the lower airways.

One of the disappointing aspects of aerosol technique is that children often appear to lose the required knack. For this reason, it is essential to check technique at each outpatient or clinic attendance. The commonest problem is late firing, so that the dose is either not drawn down into the airways or is actually and often visibly expired! Numerous interface devices have been produced in an attempt to ease the administration problem. Simple tube systems, such as the Aerospacer or even disposable items, such as cardboard tubes, may help some children as less of the drug is likely to impact on the fauces. The main reason for this is that the velocity of the aerosol drops rapidly. Firing too early or too late will still create situations in which much of the active ingredient will be lost.

Other systems (Nebuhaler and Aerochamber) have been carefully designed to provide conditions in which the active ingredient will remain virtually stationary in the body of the device for several seconds. They also incorporate one-way flap valves so that the drugs cannot be blown away (see Figure 5.5). Optimal benefit will be obtained if the children are encouraged to pant in and out of the device after several doses (up to six) have been fired into the body of the apparatus.

Many children find aerosol or powder delivery systems ineffective when airways obstruction is of sufficient severity to limit inspiratory flow rates, creating conditions in which larger proportions of the drugs will impact in the upper airways. The standard method for overcoming this problem is to deliver the $beta_2$ stimulant drug as a nebulized mist over 5–10 min using a nebulizer and compressed air source.[5] For this a gas compressor, a gas cylinder or a wall supply can be used. The major advantage of this device is that the child will then breathe in a $beta_2$-enriched environment over 5–10 min of tidal breathing. If children have severe attacks requiring frequent trips to the local hospital or clinic for nebulization therapy, it may be appropriate to provide the family with a system for domestic use.

An alternative approach is to insert the mouth of a $beta_2$ aerosol into the base of a disposable coffee cup[6] or similar device (see Figure 5.6). This can then be held loosely over the child's face and the aerosol activated up to ten times over a 2-min period (ie, allowing 10–15 s between each delivery). Although much of the drug will impact on the child's face or be lost into the surrounding air, this manoeuvre produces bronchodilatation very similar to that occurring with the nebulizer compressor system (see Figure 5.7).

Frequency of oral therapy   Side-effects, such as tachycardia and hand tremor, are likely if recommended doses are given more than four times each day. We still have little information on whether these formulations should be given regularly or only at times when symptoms are present. One study suggested that regular therapy did lead to a reduction in symptoms and better peak flow, although the benefits were small.[7] For those who wheeze only at times when they have upper respiratory tract infections, it seems reasonable to commence therapy as soon as there are signs that the child has a cold.

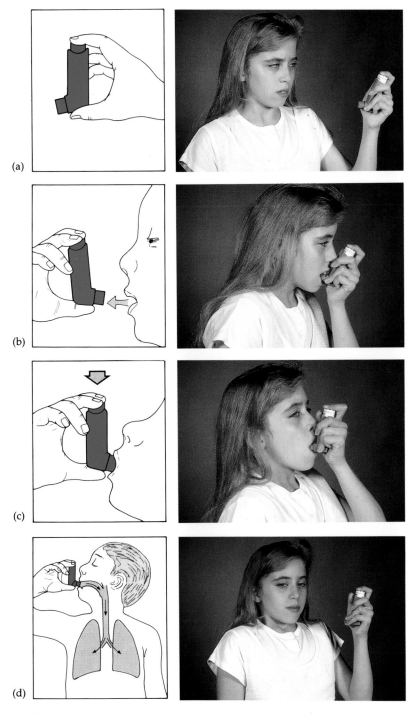

Figure 5.4 The aerosol technique. (a) The child first shakes the aerosol, then breathes out gently and places the mouthpiece of the inhaler in her mouth (b). She starts to breathe in, firing the aerosol early in the breath (c). Finally she holds the air in her lungs for several seconds before breathing out (d).

Figure 5.5 The Nebuhaler and the Aerochamber. Two interface units for use with aerosols that are suitable for children above the age of three years.

(a)   (b)

Figure 5.6 The coffee cup delivery system (a) and in use (b).

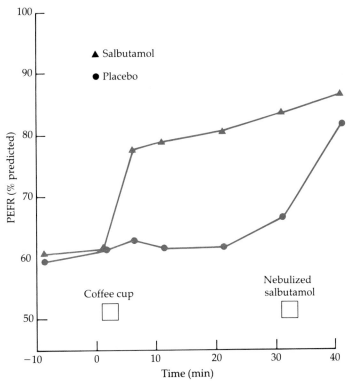

Figure 5.7 Peak flow in young asthmatic children before and after the
inhalation of ten puffs of salbutamol or placebo using a coffee cup.
Inhalation of nebulized salbutamol respirator solution had little additional
effect.

Frequency of inhalation therapy   The therapeutic/toxic ratio of inhaled therapy is
extremely high, and it is very unlikely that a child will suffer as a result of even the
gravest of overuse. The majority of aerosol canisters contain little more than the
recommended 24-hour oral dose. One hundred capsules of the powder, the usual
quantity prescribed, have a total dosage little above the recommended two-day oral
intake. It is therefore extremely unlikely for any child to develop serious side-effects,
even if aerosol canisters or powder capsule containers last only a few days. On the other
hand, such frequent use does indicate that the child's asthma is largely out of control. It
is reasonable for a child to have to use his inhalation therapy up to 4-hourly or even
3-hourly at times when the asthma is troublesome. If the inhaler fails to produce
satisfactory relief within minutes, or the improvement lasts only 1–2 hours, further
action is urgently required (see page 94). Used in this manner the inhaler not only
provides the most effective method for relieving asthma, but also provides the family
and child with an invaluable indication of the severity of the asthma attack.

   Parents and children should be encouraged to use beta$_2$ stimulants early. There is a
tendency for all therapy to be withheld 'in case the asthma gets worse'. All the evidence
we have indicates that beta$_2$ stimulants work best early in an attack and are unlikely to be
effective once there are secondary changes of mucosal oedema and intraluminal
accumulation of secretions and cellular debris.

Slow-release beta$_2$ stimulant preparations are now available. These achieve reasonable blood levels for at least 8 hours.[8] They have usually been prescribed for the treatment of nocturnal or early morning symptoms, but are probably not as useful as slow-release theophylline preparations (see below). These preparations must be swallowed and not chewed, as chewing would destroy their slow-release characteristics.

Oral theophyllines

The mode of action of theophyllines is under dispute. There is currently little evidence to support the initial claim that this group of drugs acts by inhibiting the production of phosphodiesterase, an intracellular enzyme which breaks down cyclic AMP.[8]

Although the theophyllines are bronchodilator drugs, they also have prophylactic effects and can be considered as oral alternatives to sodium cromoglycate.[9] Their main problems are potentially dangerous side-effects with a relatively low therapeutic/toxic ratio. The side-effects (see Table 5.2) include nausea, vomiting, diarrhoea, convulsions, enuresis and behaviour disturbance. There are now excellent slow-release theophylline preparations, so that for a child over the age of five years there is probably no place for syrup preparations which have therapeutic effects for only 4–6 hours. The preparations are either in the form of tablets or capsules containing slow-release minipellets.

Theophylline therapy has an important role in the management of nocturnal asthma. One capsule or tablet taken on going to bed can often provide sufficient bronchodilator effect to allow children who were previously waking virtually every night with cough and wheezing to sleep through.[10] Taken this way, they will often help children who have morning dipping with troublesome attacks of asthma at breakfast time. They can also be given as regular therapy two or three times a day, depending on the duration of action (see Table 5.3). Although there is now a preparation which produces good theophylline blood levels for at least 18 hours, information on its use in childhood asthma remains limited. Regular theophylline therapy can be supplemented by inhaled beta$_2$ stimulant drugs for breakthrough wheezing and coughing. There has been considerable debate on whether theophyllines or beta$_2$ stimulants are synergistic or purely additive, but certainly both can be given together with considerable benefit to the child.

Selection of dose   Inevitably the relatively low therapeutic/toxic ratio means that doses have to be selected with much greater care than with beta$_2$ stimulants if optimal results are to be obtained with no, or only minimal, side-effects. Unfortunately, although absorption is rapid and complete, the metabolic breakdown rate varies considerably between children and indeed at different times in the same child. Other factors can also alter the rate of breakdown, including infections and various drugs (see Table 5.4). If the child's asthma is not particularly severe, it is usually sufficient to prescribe on the cautious side, providing up to 20 mg/kg per day of theophylline equivalent. Many children will then have satisfactory control with the help of inhaled beta$_2$ stimulants as and when necessary. If the child's asthma is severe and optimal therapy is required in an attempt to keep systemic steroid requirements to a minimum, peak and trough blood levels will be required (ie, before and 4–6 hours after therapy). Since toxic effects are unlikely with blood levels of 20 μg/ml, most aim for peak levels of between 10 and

Table 5.2 Side-effects of theophylline

Nausea
Vomiting
Diarrhoea
Headache
Irritability
Insomnia
Nocturnal enuresis
Cardiac arrhythmias
Convulsions
Brain damage
Death

Table 5.3 Oral theophyllines for schoolchildren

Drug (generic name)	Formulation	Dose (total daily theophylline dose)	Frequency (dose/day)
Amino-phylline	IV injection 25 mg/ml (20 mg/ml)	5 mg/kg	Once, slowly over 15 min Maintenance dose (0.7 mg/ kg per hour)
	Sustained release tablets 100 mg (80 mg), 142 mg (90 mg) 225 mg (180 mg)	20 mg/kg	2 or 3 (for younger ages)
	Tablets 100 mg (65 mg)	20 mg/kg	Need to be given 4 times/ day
	Elixir 62.5 mg (40 mg)/ 5 ml	20 mg/kg	
Theophylline	Tablets 125 mg	20 mg/kg	Need to be given 4 times/ day
	Elixir 60 mg/5 ml	20 mg/kg	Need to be given 4 times/ day
	Sustained release capsules 60, 100, 125, 175, 200, 250, 300 mg (contents can be emptied out and used)	20 mg/kg	2 or 3 (see above)

Table 5.4 Factors leading to high serum theophylline levels

Infections
Acute hepatitis
Cholestatic jaundice
Cardiac decompensation
Cor pulmonale
Erythromycin
Troleandomycin
Cimetidine

15 µg/ml. Levels over 30 µg/ml are very likely to produce nausea, vomiting and possibly convulsions. Some children, particularly those under the age of five years, may have gastrointestinal symptoms despite normal blood levels. It is essential that the children and their parents are aware that theophyllines have been prescribed, because a potentially dangerous situation can arise if intravenous aminophylline is given to children already on optimal oral therapy. The gastrointestinal side-effects of nausea and vomiting can often be avoided if a relatively low dose is prescribed initially (ie, 10–15 mg/kg per day) and then increased at one to two week intervals with the help of blood theophylline estimations.

Sodium cromoglycate

In contrast to most other forms of treatment in asthma, recent research has made us less secure about the mode of action of sodium cromoglycate. In vitro studies have indicated that the drug does have considerable mast-cell stabilizing effects. However, other drugs which have more potent mast-cell stabilizing characteristics (eg, ketotifen) have been found to be far less effective in the prophylaxis of asthma.[11] As a result we are now less certain of the importance of the mast cell in the aetiology of asthma attacks. There is good evidence that sodium cromoglycate is an effective antiasthma agent in most children,[12] but unfortunately it is not possible to predict with any degree of certainty whether it will prove effective in any given child. The severity of allergic symptoms provides no help. Most studies suggest that sodium cromoglycate is least useful in those with the severest symptoms. In general, it seems that those who respond best are those who are most helped by theophylline therapy.[12]

Indications   Sodium cromoglycate should be given to any child whose symptoms cannot be controlled by intermittent beta$_2$ stimulant therapy alone. Some authorities advise that sodium cromoglycate should also be given to any child who requires regular beta$_2$ stimulant therapy (at least two doses per day), even if symptoms are well controlled, as this may reduce bronchial reactivity in the long term.[13]

Frequency and mode of delivery   For children under the age of seven or eight years, sodium cromoglycate is best inhaled as a powder using the Spinhaler or the more recently developed Halermatic (see Figure 5.8): both appear to be equally effective but the Halermatic is perhaps a little more convenient. There are two aerosols for the older child who has shown that he can use these devices satisfactorily (Intal and Intal 5). These deliver 1 mg and 5 mg respectively, considerably less than the 20 mg contained in the Spinhaler and Halermatic capsules. There is some evidence to suggest that the 1 mg aerosol is a little less effective than the capsule, but more information is needed.[14] Sodium cromoglycate seems to be entirely devoid of side-effects, apart from a tendency to induce coughing in those who are very sensitive to the inhalation of particulate matter. The main disadvantage is that the duration of action is relatively short, so therapy should be repeated at least three and preferably four times a day. Additional doses can be taken immediately before exercise, although sodium cromoglycate is less effective than inhaled beta$_2$ stimulants for this purpose. As with theophylline therapy, children should be encouraged to take inhaled beta$_2$ stimulants as soon as breakthrough coughing or wheezing occurs.

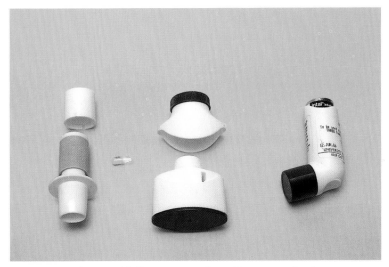

Figure 5.8 A selection of delivery systems for sodium cromoglycate. From left to right: the Spinhaler, the Halermatic and an aerosol (Intal).

Reduction of therapy   Although sodium cromoglycate seems to be entirely safe and free from dangerous side-effects, parents and children often wish to know when therapy can be reduced or discontinued. As a rule therapy will be needed for years rather than months. If beta$_2$ stimulant therapy is taken more than once or twice a week, sodium cromoglycate should be continued. If beta$_2$ stimulants have not been needed for periods longer than this, it is reasonable to try reducing the sodium cromoglycate dose to two to three times per day. If the child's condition does not deteriorate, the sodium cromoglycate can be withdrawn. It is worth warning the parents that it may be necessary to restart treatment if symptoms recur after a severe respiratory tract infection or even allergen challenge.

Topical steroids

Topical steroids have proved extremely useful in the management of children with moderate to severe asthma. They are distinguished from systemic steroid preparations by low solubility in water, so that the inhaled dose remains confined to the lung for long periods and is only relatively slowly removed by the pulmonary circulation. Their mode of action is almost certainly identical to that of the systemic steroids, producing benefit

Table 5.5 Pharmacological actions of steroids

- Stabilize membranes
- Induce synthesis of lipomodulin and therefore inhibit formation of prostaglandins and leukotrienes
- Inhibit neutrophil chemotaxis
- Reduce mediator release from inflammatory cells

by several different mechanisms (see Table 5.5). Of these, the most important are firstly their ability to generate newly synthesized proteins (macrocortin and lipomodulin) which inhibit the formation of leukotrienes, prostaglandins, thromboxanes and other metabolites of arachidonic acid, and secondly their ability to block eosinophil and neutrophil chemotaxis.

Indications   Virtually all children with asthma will respond dramatically to inhaled topical steroids.[15] Over the last few years there has been a trend to use this group of drugs more and more extensively, particularly since they can almost always be given on a simple twice-daily regime.[16] The main limiting factor on even more general use in childhood asthma has been the worry about side-effects, which so far have proved potential rather than actual. Several studies have shown that inhaled topical steroids increase the frequency with which candida can be grown from mouth and throat swabs. However, clinically troublesome thrush is rare in childhood, affecting probably less than 1 per cent of children on regular therapy. Even this responds rapidly to withdrawal of therapy or treatment with oral nystatin suspensions. There have also been worries that exposing the respiratory mucosa to topical steroids over long periods would produce atropic changes similar to those seen in the skin of patients on dermatological preparations. Although we have no information on children, lung and nasal biopsies obtained from adults who have received topical steroids for as long as three years have shown no abnormal changes on either light or electron microscopy.[17] Very occasionally a child on topical steroids develops dysphonia, which is thought to be due to paralysis of the laryngeal adductor muscles. This is usually dose-related and will disappear if the dose of topical steroids is reduced.

The more worrying hormonal effects of topical steroids are largely limited by low water solubility and the relatively small doses administered. However, if the normal recommended dose is more than doubled or trebled (eg, more than 1600 µg beclomethasone dipropionate or its equivalent per day), effects will become evident. The children then tend to have exceedingly large weight gains due to water retention and may even become slightly cushingoid. There is also evidence that these high doses interfere with the ability of the hypothalamic–pituitary–adrenal axis to respond to stress (metyrapone).[18] Fortunately there is no evidence that an adrenal crisis has occurred as a result of even very high dosage. It is possible, however, that the normal pulsatile pattern of cortical release may be affected by inhaled steroids.[19] Growth hormone secretion appears unaffected, and so far growth suppression has not been documented as a side-effect in childhood. Nevertheless it seems reasonable to restrict topical steroids to those who have relatively frequent or severe symptoms which cannot be controlled by a combination of sodium cromoglycate and beta$_2$ stimulant drugs. They are certainly indicated in any child who, despite this combination, is missing school or is unable to join in with full physical activities. Topical steroids are essential for all children who require systemic steroids regularly or frequently.

Selection   There is no evidence that any one of the topical steroids available produces superior clinical results (see Table 5.6). Beclomethasone dipropionate has the advantage that it is available as both an aerosol and a powder which can be inhaled using a rotahaler device (see page 47). Whichever drug is selected it is obviously important to ensure that inhalation technique is adequate. For those under eight years of age, and for many over, it is preferable either to commence them on beclomethasone powder or to use an interface device, such as the Aerospacer or Nebuhaler. Many authorities

Table 5.6 Topical steroid preparations for schoolchildren

Drug (generic name)	**Dose**

Beclomethasone dipropionate
   Inhaled powder
   (100, 200 μg)
   Aerosol
   (50 μg/puff)
	100–400 μg
	
	2–6 puffs

Betamethasone valerate
(give each dose 2–4 times/day)
   Aerosol
   (100 μg/puff)
	1–3 puffs

Budesonide
(give each dose 2 times/day)
   Aerosol
   (50, 200 μg/puff)
	50–200 μg

recommend that the topical steroid should be preceded by a $beta_2$ stimulant inhalation to obtain maximum bronchodilatation and thus better penetration. However, there are some children who are so well controlled by regular topical steroid therapy that this is not necessary.

Dose   For most children twice daily therapy is sufficient, using total dosage which will be entirely free from measurable hormonal effects. This can be increased to three or even four times a day if the child is receiving systemic steroids or has prolonged deterioration in his asthma control. It is again important to stress to children and their parents that $beta_2$ stimulant drugs must be taken for coughing and wheezing attacks.

The vast majority of asthmatic children who require topical steroids will get little, if any, additional benefits from taking sodium cromoglycate as well.[20] Combined therapy may reduce compliance, particularly in teenage children who are often happy to take $beta_2$ stimulants but reluctant to accept prophylactic therapy.

Systemic steroids

Although systemic steroids have the most worrying side-effects, they are also the most potent antiasthma drugs available. Systemic steroids have three main roles in childhood asthma, which are:

- As an aid to diagnosis
- In the management of acute asthma attacks
- As longterm prophylaxis.

Aid to diagnosis   As already stated, the diagnosis of asthma is almost always based on careful history and confirmed by demonstrating abnormal airways lability often as a dramatic improvement in lung function after inhaled $beta_2$ stimulants. Occasionally children present with severe and apparently persistent airways obstruction with only partial response to inhaled $beta_2$ stimulants. It is then very important both from the management and from the prognostic points of view to establish whether the child has severe irreversible airways obstruction with some degree of increased airways lability or has severe and totally reversible airways obstruction. This problem can readily be resolved by measuring lung function, preferably including body plethysmography, so that hyperinflation can be assessed, and then prescribing a ten to fourteen day course of systemic steroids (eg, prednisolone 1–2mg/kg per day and regular inhaled beta$_2$ stimulants). The lung function measurement is repeated at the end of the course. A dramatic improvement with the relief of hyperinflation and return of lung function to normal indicates that the underlying problem is asthma. Partial improvement confirms that the child has severe irreversible airways obstruction and will receive limited benefit from antiasthma therapy. These children will need further investigations in an attempt to identify the aetiology (see Table 5.7). Children responding well can often be maintained on a combination of inhaled topical steroids and beta$_2$ stimulants, if necessary with slow-release theophylline preparations.

Table 5.7 Causes of irreversible airways obstruction in childhood

Cystic fibrosis
Bronchiectasis
Obliterative bronchiolitis
α_1 Antitrypsin deficiency

The management of acute attacks In recent years there has been a considerable reluctance to prescribe systemic steroids for acute severe asthma not responding to the child's normal maintenance and beta$_2$ stimulant therapy. It is important to stress that a three to five day course is almost always entirely safe and free from side-effects provided it is not repeated too frequently (ie, more than once every two to three months), and is certainly preferable to hospital admission. As adrenal suppression does not occur over such a brief period, weaning off is unnecessary. Its only function is that parents tend to remember weaning instruction. This provides a marker of steroid therapy for doctors seeing the child in the future! There are also many asthmatic children whose control is normally satisfactory but have periods lasting weeks or months when the condition deteriorates so that they are unable to attend school or join in with full physical activities, even though they are taking their regular prophylactic and inhaled beta$_2$ stimulant therapy. It is entirely reasonable to give these children a ten to fourteen day steroid course in order to re-establish control, presumably by reducing inflammatory changes within the airways.

Longterm prophylactic therapy Regular steroid therapy is indicated only in the very occasional child who continues to have severe and disabling symptoms despite optimal conservative therapy, including inhaled topical steroids, regular inhaled beta$_2$ stimulants and slow-release theophylline preparations. They should also be considered for children who have frequent admissions to hospital and have courses of systemic steroids more often than once every one or two months. Usually it will be necessary to give a full steroid course (1–2mg/kg per day of prednisolone for ten to fourteen days). It is essential that the child is continued on a full antiasthma drug regime in an attempt to keep the systemic steroids dose, and thus the risk of side-effects, down to a minimum. This will include regular beta$_2$ stimulant therapy. This is best given by nebulizer twice a day. The child will also require maximum doses of topical steroids (eg, beclomethasone dipropionate 400 µg three to four times a day), and twice daily slow-release theophylline formulations; these should be adjusted to obtain blood levels between 10 and 20 µg/ml. The steroid can then be reduced, aiming to keep the dose down to 5 mg or at the most 10 mg of prednisolone or its equivalent on alternate days. This will reduce the side-effects. The aim must always be to wean the child totally off steroids as soon as possible, but there remain a very small number in whom continued therapy can be lifesaving. It is clearly essential to see these children regularly to assess progress, to plot growth and height and to optimize therapy.

Other drug therapy

Antihistamines have been given for many years. There is, however, no evidence that this group of drug has any effect on symptoms or lung function when taken orally. Inhaled antihistamines do produce bronchodilatation in children with asthma but this effect is relatively weak compared to beta$_2$ stimulant therapy.[21] One study failed to show any improvement in control when inhaled clemastine was added to conventional therapy and the results compared with inhaled placebo preparations.[22] There is little, if any, place for the use of antihistamines in asthma, although they are of course useful for associated hay fever symptoms.

Ketotifen is a potent antihistamine which has strong in vitro mast-cell stabilizing characteristics. As it is taken orally and lasts for 12 hours, it would seem to represent a considerable advance in the prophylaxis of asthma. Unfortunately there are now a number of well-controlled clinical trials which have failed to show measurable benefit.[23] Other and perhaps less satisfactory trials have suggested that improvement may take as long as three months to show. The fact that this drug appears to be so much less effective than sodium cromoglycate raises the suggestion that sodium cromoglycate may have other actions in the lung, in addition to its effects on the mast cell.

CHILDREN AGED TWO TO FIVE YEARS

Bronchodilator drugs

Oral therapy Although asthmatic children between the ages of two and five years do obtain relief from oral beta$_2$ stimulants, response is slow and tends to be incomplete (see Figure 5.9). Nevertheless this route of therapy (syrup) is both convenient and often adequate for children who wheeze infrequently and often only at times when they have signs of an upper respiratory tract infection. Side-effects are relatively rare for this age group and doses can be repeated at 4–6 hour intervals if necessary (see Table 5.8).

Inhalation therapy As in older children, inhalation therapy provides a more satisfactory alternative with rapid and often dramatic relief of airways obstruction. Most children over the age of three or three-and-a-half can use powder delivery systems (Rotahaler) after a little practice. The doses recommended by drug firms can, if necessary, be doubled with complete safety as even then they will not exceed 20 per cent

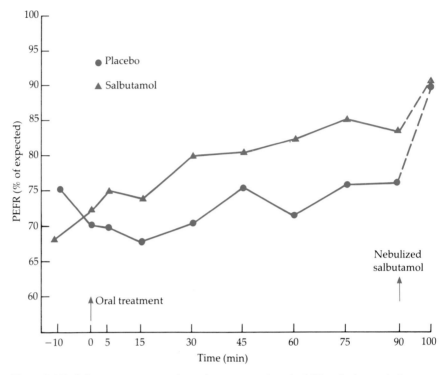

Figure 5.9 Peak flow measurements in twelve young asthmatic children before and after salbutamol and placebo syrup. Response is relatively slow and undramatic compared to the improvement after inhalation of nebulized salbutamol (2.5 mg in 2 ml water).

of the standard oral dose. For many children, even those with quite frequent asthma attacks, this form of therapy is sufficient to ensure that they lead relatively normal lives. Aerosol devices with simple tube interface units are not particularly helpful; preschool children tend to blow the dose out at the open end. The more sophisticated Aerochamber and Nebuhalers can be used by some children as young as three years of age, who can be encouraged to pant in and out through the one-way valve system. Even in these young children it is entirely satisfactory to fire the aerosol canister into the device chamber between two and six times. The coffee-cup delivery system (see page 50) is suitable for all children over the age of two years. The aerosol can again be fired between five and ten times (allowing approximately 10 s between each activation) with complete safety, while holding the open end of the cup loosely over the child's mouth and nose. This system also provides a useful back-up facility for times when those normally able to use powder delivery systems have such severe airways obstruction that they are unable to generate adequate inspiratory flow rates.

The nebulizer compressor system remains the most effective delivery technique[24] and should be provided to families whose child has asthma attacks necessitating frequent trips to the local clinic or hospital for nebulization therapy. Ultrasonic systems should be avoided, as these may induce rather than relieve airways obstruction.

Table 5.8 Beta₂ adrenergic stimulant drugs in children aged two to five years

Drug (generic name)	Formulation	Dose	Frequency (dose/day)
Fenoterol	Respirator solution (0.5%) (dilute 4–20 times)	0.5–1 mg	up to 6
Pirbuterol	Elixir (7.5 mg/5 ml)	3.75 mg	up to 4
Reproterol	Elixir (10 mg/5 ml) Tablets (20 mg) Respirator solution (0.1%) (dilute 4 times)	5 mg 10 mg 5 mg	up to 4 up to 4 up to 6
Rimiterol	Respirator solution (0.5%) (dilute 2 times)	6.25 mg	up to 6
Salbutamol	Elixir (2 mg/5 ml) Tablets (2 mg) Inhaler powder (200–400 µg) Respirator solution (0.1%) (nebules) IV/IM injection (50 µg/ml)	2 mg 2 mg 200 µg 2.5 mg 4–6 µg/kg	up to 4 up to 4 up to 6 up to 6 single dose
Terbutaline	Elixir (1.5 mg/5 ml) Aerosol spacer (250 µg) Respirator solution (2.5 mg/ml) IV/IM injection (500 µg/ml)	1.5 mg 1–2 puffs 1.25 mg 10 µg/kg	up to 4 up to 16 up to 6 single dose

Ipratropium bromide   Although ipratropium bromide is an effective bronchodilator agent in children between the ages of three and five years (see Figure 5.10), its place in clinical management has yet to be defined. It is a selective anticholinergic drug which blocks the parasympathetic bronchoconstrictor response and has relatively little effect on heart rate or secretions. It may be worth trying in young children with severe asthma who require systemic steroids continuously or regularly in an attempt to improve control.

Theophylline therapy

There is also good evidence that preschool asthmatic children respond well to theophylline preparations (see Figure 5.11). The syrup preparations have the disadvantage that effective blood levels are only maintained for 4–6 hours and so therapy will need to be repeated three to four times a day.[25] Alternatively, theophylline can be prescribed as slow-release mini-pellets inside gelatine capsules. The pellets can be tipped out on to a teaspoon containing a sweetener, such as jam, and taken two or three times a day. This is particularly useful for those who have nocturnal symptoms. At times when the child has coughing or wheeezing, beta₂ stimulants can also be given either orally or by inhalation. If the child's asthma is not particularly troublesome, it is reasonable to aim for suboptimal therapy, giving the child a maximum of 20–24mg/kg per 24 hours with added beta₂ stimulant therapy as and when necessary, without resorting to blood level measurements. For those whose asthma is more troublesome,

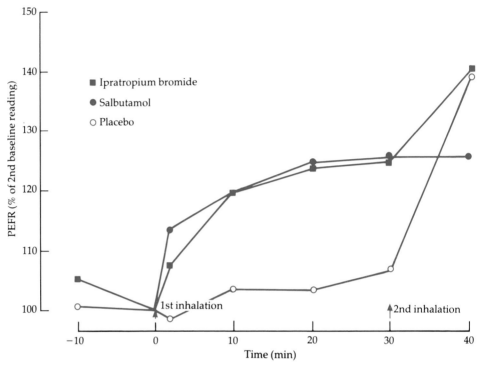

Figure 5.10 Bronchodilator effects of inhaled ipratropium bromide and salbutamol in asthmatic children aged three to five years. The effect of the ipratropium bromide is as great but a little slower in onset.

blood levels are necessary and should be obtained 2–3 hours after treatment so that dosage can be adjusted to obtain maximum benefit.

Sodium cromoglycate

Preschool children who have persistent symptoms or frequent attacks of asthma—at least one a month—and who do not respond dramatically to beta$_2$ stimulants, should be commenced on inhaled sodium cromoglycate. Some children obtain sufficient benefit by using the Spinhaler or Halermatic device but the large majority will require nebulizer/compressor systems, so that they can inhale the sodium cromoglycate as a mist over 5–10 min, three to four times a day. This has proved a highly effective form of therapy,[26] reducing symptoms and the need for frequent hospital admissions. Beta$_2$ stimulant respirator solution can be added to the sodium cromoglycate solution as and when necessary. It is then preferable to use the relatively concentrated formulations available (eg, salbutamol, 5 mg/ml) so that the volume of the solution is increased by only about 0.5 ml. This form of therapy appears to be effective throughout the two to five year age range and is almost always tolerated even by the youngest. It is an advantage if the child is weaned on to sodium cromoglycate powder or inhaled topical steroids before going to school (ie, at the age of approximately four-and-a-half years). Some children

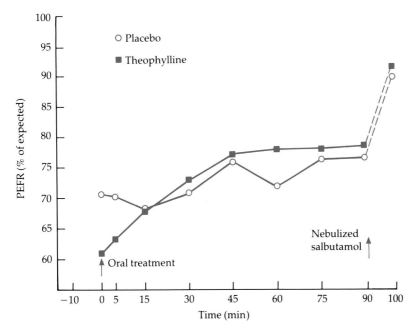

Figure 5.11 Bronchodilator response to theophylline syrup and placebo in asthmatic children aged three to five years. Nebulized salbutamol led to a further improvement in lung function.

with infrequent but severe cold-related symptoms can be managed by commencing the nebulized sodium cromoglycate and beta$_2$ stimulant as soon as signs of an impending upper respiratory tract infection show themselves.

Topical steroids

Topical steroids are certainly effective in children as young as three years, and should be considered for any child who continues to have troublesome symptoms, perhaps with frequent hospital admissions, despite nebulized sodium cromoglycate and beta$_2$ stimulant therapy. Some will be able to inhale beclomethasone dipropionate powder from a Rotahaler, taking this therapy (100–200 µg) two or even three times a day. A smaller number can inhale either beclomethasone dipropionate or budesonide aerosol by panting in and out of a Volumatic or Aerochamber device. Even so, it will usually be necessary for the child to have access to a nebulizer so that beta$_2$ stimulant therapy can be inhaled as a mist at times when the child's asthma is particularly troublesome.

Recently a topical steroid suspension of beclomethasone dipropionate has become available. Although this does appear to have some benefit to some children, the overall response to this preparation is less dramatic.[27,28] The doses delivered are smaller, even though the volumes which need to be nebulized are relatively large, often over 3 ml. Nevertheless, it is certainly worth trying on any child whose asthma is inadequately controlled and who is too young or immature to cope with the powder delivery system.

There is little doubt that further improvement in control arises as soon as the child is sufficiently coordinated to start using the powder delivery system.

Systemic steroids

Systemic steroids tend to be used rather more frequently in the two to five year age group. The reasons for this are partly that control is more difficult with topical steroids and partly that it is generally envisaged that as delivery systems present less of a problem by the age of four or five years, the child is unlikely to be dependent on systemic steroids for too long a period.

As in older children, systemic steroids have three roles:

Diagnostic   As lung function assessment is more difficult in these children, assessment of response to bronchodilator drug and hence confirmation of the diagnosis of asthma is more difficult. In those over the age of three to three-and-a-half years, it is often possible to measure peak flow before and after bronchodilator therapy, with a sufficient degree of confidence. Under this age, and indeed for some older children, information can only be obtained after sedation during an attack (see page 102) using sophisticated facilities which are not generally available. If there is doubt about the diagnosis despite a careful history and a trial of beta$_2$ stimulant therapy, it is entirely reasonable to prescribe a ten to fourteen day course of systemic steroids (eg, prednisolone 1–2 mg/kg per day) as once or twice daily therapy and assess the child clinically at the end of this period. A persistence of symptoms makes it extremely unlikely that asthma is responsible for much, if any, of the underlying pathology.

Intermittent courses   There are a significant number of asthmatic children who, despite having nebulization therapy immediately available at home, have attacks sufficiently severe to require admission to hospital virtually every time they have an upper respiratory tract infection. Often there is a 24–48 hour period between the onset of the runny nose and the start of asthma symptoms. It is then often possible to abort these by commencing a three or five day course of prednisolone, using again 1–2 mg/kg per day. As in older children, side-effects are extremely unlikely, provided that courses are not repeated at less than monthly intervals.

Continuous therapy   The number of children between the ages of two and five years who require continuous systemic steroids should be extremely small. The aim should be to keep these children on a maximum of 5 mg of prednisolone on alternative days if this is possible. These children will also need to be on regular nebulization therapy with sodium cromoglycate and beta$_2$ stimulants three to four times a day and maximal theophylline therapy, aiming always to wean the child off the systemic steroids. There will inevitably be times when higher doses are needed, but these should be reduced as soon as symptom control permits.

CHILDREN UNDER TWO YEARS OF AGE

Drug therapy is a much greater problem for children under the age of two years.

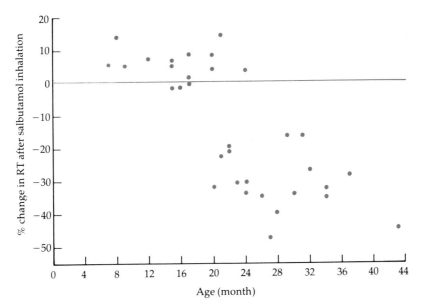

Figure 5.12 Effects of inhaled beta$_2$ stimulants (salbutamol 2.5 mg) on total respiratory resistance. No child under twenty months showed a significant improvement (ie a fall in RT).

Beta$_2$ stimulant therapy

As a rule beta$_2$ stimulants do not produce bronchodilatation until the age of fifteen or even eighteen months (see Figure 5.12).[29] The reason for this remains obscure. Smooth muscle is certainly present, although perhaps in smaller quantities than in later childhood. Beta$_2$ receptor sites have also been identified in lung tissue although again probably in smaller numbers than later in life. Whether these beta$_2$ receptor sites are fully functional is at present unknown. A further suggestion is that as the airways are relatively narrower, mucosal oedema may account for a higher proportion of the airways resistance. Recent information indicates that even in the first few months of life bronchoconstrictor agents, such as carbachol, histamine[30] and ultrasonic water, will induce bronchoconstriction and that these bronchoconstrictor responses can be blocked by prior treatment with beta$_2$ stimulants.[31] Whatever the mechanism, in practical terms very few wheezy infants under the age of fifteen months will receive any measurable benefit from bronchodilator drugs. However, even in the first year of life, it is certainly worth trying beta$_2$ stimulants on those who have troublesome wheezing, giving therapy as either oral syrup, nebulized solutions or aerosols delivered using the coffee-cup system (see page 50). Those over the age of eighteen months will almost always respond in an identical manner to older asthmatic children and should receive therapy whenever symptoms are present.

Ipratropium bromide Nebulized ipratropium bromide has an interesting role in the management of wheezing in infancy. Approximately 40 per cent[32] of wheezy babies in the first year of life respond to nebulized ipratropium bromide with dramatic clinical and

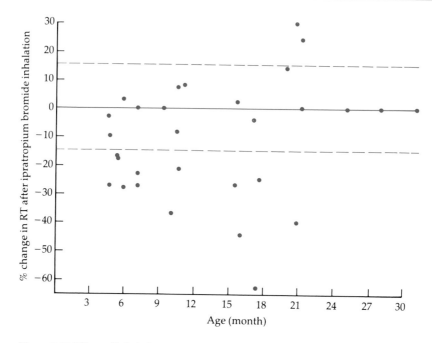

Figure 5.13 Effects of inhaled ipratropium bromide on total respiratory resistance. Forty per cent of children responded (with a fall) at all ages.

lung function improvements within 5–10 min (see Figure 5.13). Why ipratropium bromide should prove effective in situations where beta$_2$ stimulants are of no measurable value remains unknown. Ipratropium bromide, an anticholinergic agent, appears to act on the central rather than the peripheral airways. Although we do not have precise information on the distribution of airways obstruction in babies with asthma, hyperinflation certainly occurs early, indicating that the small airways are involved. Our information on optimal dosage is also sketchy but 125 µg in 2 ml of saline can be nebulized at 3–4 hour intervals without obvious side-effects. Alternatively the ipratropium bromide aerosol can be used with the help of the coffee-cup delivery system. Up to five puffs (200 µg) can be given allowing at least 10 s between each activation. Why some children respond and others do not also remains a mystery. There do not seem to be any relationships between response and history of allergy, or family history of atopy, or age.[33] Therapeutic trial is currently the only way to identify responders.

Theophylline

What information is available suggests that oral theophyllines are no more effective than beta$_2$ stimulants in relieving bronchoconstriction in the first year of life. Whether they have a place in the second year has not yet been established. Theophylline syrup is certainly prescribed quite widely for this group of children, but we need more information before its place can be properly defined.

Sodium cromoglycate

There are now two studies[33,34] which indicate that sodium cromoglycate, given as a nebulized solution, is an effective prophylactic agent in children in the second year of life but is of little value in the first twelve months. Again the reason for this is unknown. It is certainly worth trying children with troublesome recurrent or persistent asthma symptoms not adequately controlled by nebulized beta$_2$ stimulants on nebulized sodium cromoglycate (20 mg), given three or if necessary four times a day, once they are over the age of twelve months. The difficulties of administration and the poor results found do not justify its use in children under this age.

Topical steroids

Although a number of children under the age of two years have been given nebulized beclomethasone dipropionate suspension, our information on its place in therapy remains anecdotal and not very encouraging. Again it is worth trying in the children whose symptoms cannot be controlled by a beta$_2$ stimulant, ipratropium bromide or sodium cromoglycate, but a useful response is very unlikely in the first year of life.

Systemic steroids

There are now two control trials[35,36] which have failed to demonstrate any benefit from systemic steroids in the first twelve months of life. One study[36] found that after a week of systemic steroids there were as many children still wheezing in the treated group as in the control placebo-treated group. But there was a tendency for improvement to occur earlier in those between the age of twelve and eighteen months. It may be that some children do benefit before this age, but in the first eighteen months of life a failure to respond to systemic steroids certainly does not exclude the diagnosis of asthma. One study has suggested that although beta$_2$ stimulants and systemic steroids are ineffective in the first year of life when given independently, combined therapy may give some benefit.[35] There are also some exerimental data on lymphocytes which suggest that systemic steroids may activate the beta$_2$ receptor sites, allowing a bronchodilator response to occur.

Practical approach

Children over the age of eighteen months are very likely to respond to beta$_2$ stimulants. This can be given in syrup form if the asthma is relatively mild or by inhalation using a nebulizer or coffee-cup system for those with more troublesome symptoms. For children under this age, it is worth trying inhaled beta$_2$ stimulants and assessing the response. If this produces no benefit, try nebulized ipratropium bromide during an attack of coughing and wheezing. If this too is ineffective and the child is under the age of one year, it is unlikely that any therapy will help. Fortunately, severe life-threatening asthma is extremely rare at this age and the large majority of children are remarkably happy despite their symptoms. Parents can be reassured that the attacks will be easier to cope with once the child is a little older. It is probably worth trying beta$_2$ stimulants again once the child is twelve months old, and if necessary to repeat these therapeutic trials at monthly intervals. For those over one year of age, nebulized sodium cromoglycate can be a useful prophylactic agent and should be given to all children with troublesome symptoms which are difficult to control.

PRACTICAL POINTS

- An assessment of severity is essential so that treatment can be tailored to the child's needs.

- Parental and child education are vital for good control.

- Bronchodilator drugs (beta$_2$ stimulants) are more effective and act much faster if inhaled rather than swallowed.

- Children under the age of eight years can rarely use aerosols.

- Slow-release theophylline preparations are useful for nocturnal symptoms but have a low therapeutic/toxic ratio.

- Sodium cromoglycate is an effective prophylactic agent in approximately 70 per cent of asthmatic children.

- Inhaled topical steroids should be given to children who have troublesome symptoms despite sodium cromoglycate and beta$_2$ stimulants.

- Systemic steroids are safe only if given for short, infrequent courses.

- Children aged two to five years respond well to all anti-asthma treatments. The main problem is that of drug delivery.

- Nebulizers have a major role to play.

- Children under the age of one year rarely respond to beta$_2$ stimulants, sodium cromoglycate or even systemic steroids. Approximately 40 per cent will benefit from ipratropium bromide.

6
Allergen avoidance and desensitization

AVOIDANCE OF ALLERGENS

Although most severe attacks of asthma are brought on by viral infection, the large majority of asthmatic children have atopic tendencies, often with eczema and hay fever. A high proportion, 80 per cent aged three-and-a-half years[1] and over 90 per cent by the age of ten,[2] will have multiple positive skin tests. Those tests most likely to be positive are house dust, house dust mite, cat fur and pollens (see Table 6.1). If contact with furry animals, such as cats or dogs, induces an immediate reaction with rhinitis, coughing and wheezing, the parents and sometimes a little more reluctantly their asthmatic children will take action to reduce contact to a minimum.

Unfortunately allergens can also work more subtly and may then produce symptoms only when there are other adverse factors, such as an infection or possible changes in environmental factors. Continuous contact with allergens, such as house dust mite and animals furs in the home, can also be responsible for background asthma symptoms without obviously triggering severe asthma attacks. As already stated, skin tests are rarely useful in these situations and although bronchial provocation tests may help identify important sensitivities, these are cumbersome and not without their dangers (see page 42). For this reason allergen avoidance represents the only practical way of sorting out the relevance of different allergens. This too is not without its problems.

Animal furs

All furry domestic animals, including hamsters, gerbils, rabbits and rats, can act as allergens. If a child's asthma is relatively difficult to control with frequent or persistent symptoms, it may be worth removing the animal from the home, if present. This is not difficult if the animal is kept in a cage, like a rabbit or a guinea pig. Cats and dogs present greater problems. It is sometimes worth finding a friend or relative who is prepared to foster the animal for a minimum of two months, and preferably longer, to see whether the child's symptoms improve significantly. In practice, removal of the animal may produce more emotional problems which will disguise any improvement in control. If the child's asthma is not a major problem, it may be inappropriate to take this action. It is, however, preferable to advise parents with asthmatic children not to acquire any furry pets and thus avoid this situation.

As many children are also sensitive to bird's feathers, parents should be advised to replace any feather-filled pillows, duvets or eiderdowns with synthetic substitutes.

Table 6.1 The skin tests likely to be positive

House dust
House dust mite
Grass pollen
Cat
Dog
Tree pollens
Aspergillus fumigatus

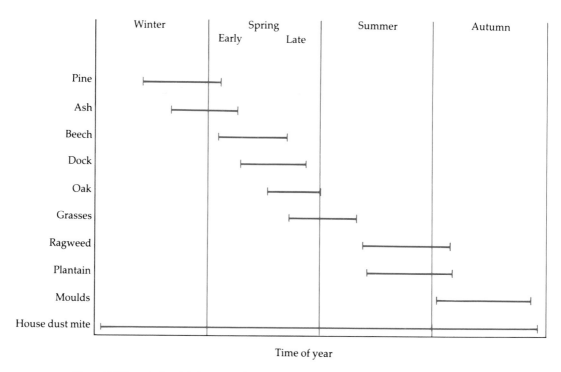

Figure 6.1 The relationship between the time of year and allergic responses to allergens.

Pollens and moulds

It is usually easy to identify from the history those children who are sensitive to pollen and mould as they will almost always have hay fever symptoms during the appropriate season (see Figure 6.1). It is obviously reasonable to advise these children not to go out in the fields when pollen is abundant, and probably advisable to keep bedroom windows closed when the pollen or mould count is high.

House dust and house dust mite

As so many asthmatic children are sensitive to house dust, and in particular to the faeces of the house dust mite (*Dermatophagoides pteronyssinus*), it seems sensible to reduce house dust to a minimum, particularly in the bedroom. This involves vacuuming the bedroom carpet, curtains and furniture regularly, at least three times a week. It is unlikely that replacing carpets with a hard floor covering is an advantage, as the carpets do at least tend to trap the house dust. Measurements which aim to reduce the house dust mite population include replacing woollen blankets with cotton or synthetic ones which can be washed frequently, placing a sheet of polythene between the undersheet and mattress to isolate the mites in the body of the bed, and vacuuming the sheets and the blankets regularly. There is also a new antifungal preparation (Tymasil) which can be sprayed on the bed. This apparently reduces the house dust mite population because fungi are needed to help predigest the skin scales which form the mites' main diet. Guideline sheets are available which can be handed out to parents (see Table 6.2). Most open studies have shown that these measures lead to an improvement in control in at least some children. Carefully conducted studies in which control groups are included are less convincing. For example, one group in Bristol sent a nurse to carry out the bedroom measures. In the placebo group the vacuum was inactivated, although the

---

Table 6.2 Measures to help reduce house dust mite sensitivity

In the bedroom
Essential measures:
- Remove feather pillows and eiderdowns and replace with synthetic ones, eg, Dunlopillo, Dacron or Terylene
- Vacuum the mattress, pillows and around the base of the bed or divan thoroughly. Enclose the mattress top surface and sides in a plastic cover.
- Damp-dust the plastic mattress cover daily.
- Change and wash pillow cases, sheets, underblankets, and vacuum bed base weekly. Keep your child out of the room while cleaning.
- Remove stuffed toys as far as possible, allowing only washable ones in the bedroom. Wash them frequently, especially if taken to bed.

Desirable measures
- Replace woollen blankets with synthetic or cotton cellular quilts or blankets, and wash frequently.
- Use light washable curtains and wash frequently.
- Use a vacuum cleaner with a disposable bag.
- Note: if the room is shared, all other beds must be treated in the same way. Allow your child to have a room of his own if possible.

In other rooms
- Vacuum upholstered furniture twice a week, especially headrests, arms and edges of seats.

On holiday
- Try to apply the same measures in rented houses, caravans and spare bedrooms as these often have a high mite count, especially if damp and infrequently used. It may be advisable to take the child's mattress cover and bedding with you, if possible.
- Mites occur all over the world, except at high altitudes.

motor continued to run. Both groups found the same degree of improvement! The reason for this seems to be that, although these measures reduce the mite population, total eradication seems to be extremely difficult and numbers increase as soon as vigilance is reduced. It seems reasonable at least to try out the recommendations, and to ensure that the bedroom is not damp, as this provides conditions particularly favourable to the house dust mite.

Food allergy

Only the role of immunotherapy generates more controversy than the place of food allergy in the management of childhood asthma. Most physicians fall into one of two groups—those who consider that food allergy is central to asthma in most children and those who 'know' that, with rare exceptions, food is irrelevant. The truth almost certainly lies somewhere between these two extremes.

One of the main problems in identifying the relative importance of food allergens is that there is no satisfactory test other than measuring response to withdrawal and then challenging at least twice under double-blind control conditions.[3] Skin tests have proved unhelpful, as many children who have no symptoms have positive skin tests and others who have proven sensitivity have negative skin reactions. As a result, the incidence and relative importance of food allergy in the asthmatic childhood population remains unknown.

There are a few children in whom the diagnosis is simple. These children have severe urticaria of the face and lip, often followed by angioneurotic oedema, rhinitis and asthma symptoms within minutes of eating particular items of food, for example, eggs and fish (see Table 6.3). Parents soon learn to identify the offending foods and take appropriate action, although sometimes it is not possible to avoid offending items totally. Where the reaction to food is less dramatic, identifying oral allergens is much more difficult. It is particularly a problem if the items, for example, dairy products, are taken daily or on a regular basis. Problems are compounded by the fact that there may well be a considerable delay between the ingestion of the food and the onset of symptoms.

Some interesting recent work has shown that intake of allergens such as Coca Cola or other fizzy drinks may have no measurable effects on lung function, even though the parents and children claim that wheezing and coughing often comes on within hours of ingestion.[4] Histamine sensitivity is increased, however, indicating that although airways calibre may not have changed, airways lability has altered and additional stimuli, either cold air or exercise, are then more likely to produce symptoms (see Figure 6.2). This may provide a useful tool for assessing sensitivities.

There are three groups of parents who seek advice on the role of food sensitivity:

- Those who have appropriately identified food items which trigger off immediate allergic reactions, including asthma
- Those whose children have severe asthma, responding poorly to drug therapy, and who are desperately anxious to explore all possible avenues
- Those who have been convinced that food allergy is a major factor, often as a result of discussion with friends or relatives or from reading dramatic reports in the lay press.

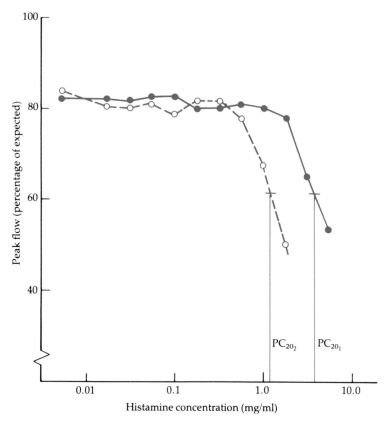

Figure 6.2 Histamine challenge before (●–●) and after (o–o) drinking Coca Cola. The baseline lung function is unchanged but the PC_{20} is reduced.

Table 6.3 Common food allergens

Dairy products
Eggs
Nuts (peanuts)
Chocolate
Colouring (tartrazine)

This third group is the most worrying, as there is a tendency for them to withdraw more and more items of food. Sometimes foods are incriminated because a spontaneous improvement coincides with the withdrawal of a particular food. Often foods are not reintroduced, even if there has been no improvement, so that eventually the child may be locked into a diet of boiled rice and little else.

Food allergy should certainly be taken seriously when parents have observed a generalized allergic reaction to specific foods, or have noticed that asthma attacks come on only after a particular food item. Other symptoms such as recurrent diarrhoea and

Table 6.4 Symptoms compatible with food allergy

Urticaria	Headache
Angioneurotic oedema	Altered behaviour
Rhinitis	Vomiting
Sinusitis	Abdominal pain
Wheeze	Diarrhoea

vomiting, are suggestive features (see Table 6.4). Children who have asthma symptoms alone and no obvious history are least likely to benefit from food exclusion.

The items most likely to produce symptoms are colouring matter, particularly tartrazine, dairy products and eggs. Tartrazine can be a major problem because it is present in many frozen, tinned and bottled foods to improve their appearance. It is often found in fruit squashes (not juices) and in other synthetic soft drinks. In the past it has also been incorporated into a number of drug preparations!

The importance of milk sensitivity in wheezing in infancy generates a great deal of controversy. Some authorities claim that it rarely, if ever, occurs when other symptoms are absent. Many parents, no doubt spurred on by the failure of the doctors to prescribe drugs which in any way modify the cause of the attacks, often try the child on goats' milk or soya milk preparations in desperation.[7]

Practical approach

If there are sufficient indications or considerable parental pressure to investigate the role of food allergens in a child, the first action after taking a careful history is to withdraw all dairy products. These obviously include milk, butter, cheese and yoghurt. Many margarines include some butter, so advice from a dietitian is required. It is important to ensure that the child is not receiving dairy products in cooked items, such as biscuits and cakes. If the child's condition improves, try reintroducing milk on an open basis. If there has been no improvement despite two or three weeks withdrawal of dairy products, try removing eggs from the diet as well. If this too is ineffective, tartrazine and other colouring matters should be withdrawn.

The next step usually involves admitting the child to a ward and commencing him on a low-allergen diet consisting of boiled rice and lamb or chicken. This will need to be maintained for at least seven days. If this coincides with improvement, then items of food can be added every three or four days until symptom deterioration occurs (see Table 6.5). This is essential, as admission to hospital may thus lead to an improvement in asthma symptoms due to factors unrelated to food allergy. Once there has been an apparent response, this should again be withdrawn for several days and the child then challenged with capsules containing placebo and active ingredient and the response noted. It may be necessary to repeat this once more. This is inevitably a very time-consuming exercise, and one that is not often popular with children. It is also important to remember that children can lose their sensitivities to foods, so it is worth trying to reintroduce items gradually after one or two years withdrawal, if accidents have not already indicated that the child is tolerant to the offending item. This approach will identify important allergens, but only occasionally does it lead to dramatic improvement, so that parents must be warned against over-optimistic expectations. It is

Table 6.5 Items permitted on a low allergen diet

Rice	Margarine (butter-free)
Chicken	Honey
Gluten-free bread	Cane sugar
Olive oil	Salt

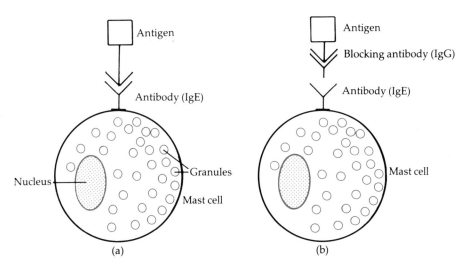

Figure 6.3 In atopy (a) the allergen combines with the antibody attached to the mast cell. Blocking antibodies (b) may prevent this.

essential that a dietitian is involved in this process, otherwise the child may suffer as a result of a dietary deficiency problem. Often added calcium and vitamins will be required.

DESENSITIZATION

As allergy induces symptoms in so many asthmatic children, any form of therapy which reduces sensitivity would seem to have a great deal to offer. For this reason, courses of desensitizing injections have been available for many years. It has been generally accepted that desensitization acts by stimulating the reticuloendothelial system to generate relatively high levels of IgG antibody against the offending antigen.[5] These antibodies will then be available to combine with the antigen as it invades the respiratory or gastrointestinal tract, so that the allergen is then no longer able to interact with IgE antibodies and so trigger off mediator release (see Figure 6.3).

The popularity of desensitization injections is due largely to dramatic anecdotal experiences. Carefully controlled double-blind trials produce less obvious benefit. A year-long study was carried out on fifty-one asthmatic children attending the Hospital for Sick Children in London.[6] All had severe symptoms and showed strongly positive reactions to bronchial provocation with house dust mite antigen. Half received twice weekly injections of a relatively pure house dust mite antigen, and half saline under double-blind conditions. Both groups showed striking improvement in symptoms and twice daily peak flows over the study period. The only significant differences between those receiving active treatment and the control were that they required less additional antiasthma therapy and, on repeat bronchial provocation, showed a reduction in the incidence of delayed reactions. No IgG blocking antibody could be demonstrated at the end of the trial. Benefit occurred least in those with the severest symptoms, and no measurable improvement could be detected one year later.[7] Further studies have produced similar results.

The present state of desensitization is that many of the dramatic responses in the past were probably largely placebo reactions. There seems little doubt that the treatment does have a measurable effect, but is not strikingly better than placebo therapy. This may in part be due not only to the lack of highly effective antigen preparations or to our lack of knowledge of the immunological changes occurring during this therapy, but also to the fact that, in many children, allergy is only one of a number of important bronchoconstrictor triggers.

Desensitization is an unpleasant form of therapy, and reactions are not uncommon.[8] But these are usually mild, with localized erythema and swelling. Very occasionally a child develops a generalized anaphylactic reaction, which tragically can prove fatal. For these reasons the place of desensitization in asthma is limited. There is certainly no evidence to support its use with mould or food sensitivity.

Indications

Desensitization therapy should be considered only for children whose asthma cannot be relatively well controlled with a combination of inhaled beta$_2$ stimulants, inhaled topical steroids and, if necessary, slow-release theophylline preparations. There should be strong information from the history to suggest that there is only one or at the most two allergens which play a major role in the child's symptoms. This should be confirmed by bronchial challenge rather than depending on a skin or nasal provocation test. It is preferable for the child to be admitted to hospital for the night after provocation as there may be a severe delayed reaction. Only if bronchial provocation tests demonstrate that there is a high degree of allergen sensitivity should desensitization be considered. The practice of prescribing multiple allergen injections on the basis of numerous skin tests is now indefensible.

Procedure Desensitizing injections should only be given under conditions where facilities are available for treating anaphylaxis (see Table 6.6). The pattern of injection depends on the allergen used, but usually the child will need at least six injections at one to two week intervals, followed by monthly maintenance injections, using the peak concentration for an undetermined period. Pollen injections can be limited to three, again at one to two week intervals, ensuring that the course is finished well before the onset of the pollen season.

Table 6.6 Facilities needed prior to giving desensitization injections

- Adrenaline 1:1000 (SC or IM)
- Antihistamines (IV or IM)
- Systemic steroids
  Oxygen
  IV Fluids
  Facilities for intubation
  (● = Essential)

Oral desensitization

Recently there have been claims that desensitization is effective if the antigens are taken by mouth. This has the major advantage that any reaction is likely to be limited to the gastrointestinal tract, and probably totally eliminates the risk of anaphylaxis. Controlled information is still very limited. What double-blind studies have been carried out are not very encouraging.

PRACTICAL POINTS

- Although viral infections are responsible for most severe prolonged attacks, allergy does have an important role.

- Sometimes the association is masked, as the allergen may increase airways lability rather than alter baseline airways resistance.

- House dust mite avoidance measures, although worth trying if the asthma is severe, are often disappointing.

- Often food allergies can only be identified by an elimination diet followed by challenges performed under double-blind conditions.

- Food items most likely to produce symptoms are preservatives, including tartrazine, dairy products and eggs.

- Desensitization injections are essentially dangerous and rarely justified.

7
The child and his asthma

Many children with asthma are still referred to physiotherapy departments. Several possible reasons may be put forward for this course of action:

- To help clear secretions
- To strengthen the respiratory muscles by breathing exercises
- To provide the child with an efficient pattern of breathing that can be used during acute attacks of asthma
- To reduce chest wall deformity.

Clearance of secretions   There is clear post mortem evidence that secretions accumulate in the airways during attacks of asthma, whether these are acute or persistent.[1] This inevitably contributes to the degree of airways obstruction, so it seems reasonable that these children should receive physiotherapy at times when they are unwell. Unfortunately there is no evidence that this line of therapy is particularly helpful except in situations where the accumulations of secretions have led to collapse of a segment or lobe (see Figure 7.1). It is not uncommon for the right middle lobe to collapse, leading to persistence of symptoms in the child who is otherwise quite well between acute attacks. In this situation physiotherapy has a major role to play and parents should receive thorough instruction, so that they can provide chest percussion and postural drainage on a twice-daily basis in addition to regular visits to a physiotherapy department. Physiotherapy may actually induce further bronchoconstriction, so should always be preceded by inhaled beta$_2$ stimulants, preferably from a nebulizer/compressor system.

Strengthening respiratory muscles   Although parents often state that their asthmatic children have 'weak chests', the increased work needed to sustain a child through an acute asthma attack is far more likely to increase respiratory muscle strength than any breathing exercises devised by even the most skilled physiotherapist! Children with asthma are able to generate high intrathoracic pressures against an external obstruction and, when well, often have supernormal lung function.

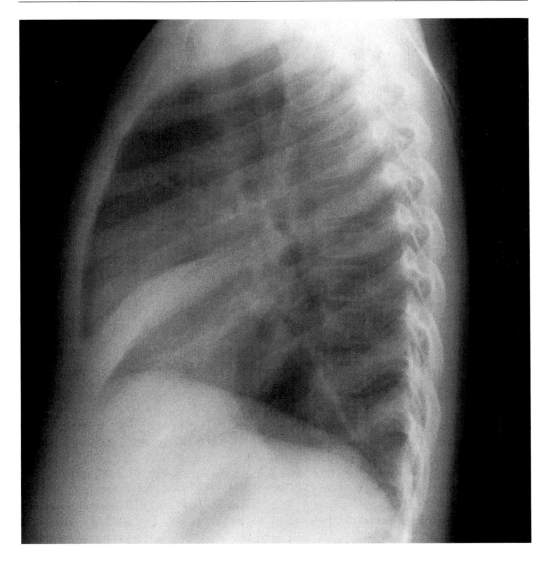

Figure 7.1 A lateral chest x-ray showing resistant collapse of right middle lobe in a five-year-old child with persistent asthma.

Controlled breathing   As already described, one effect of increased airways obstruction is to increase the time needed for expiration. The accessory respiratory muscles, including the abdominal wall, help by contracting during expiration. This inevitably has the effect of producing dynamic compression in the airways, further increasing the degree of obstruction. Not unnaturally some children panic during attacks, tending to breathe out at fast rates generating very high expiratory pressures and thus further increasing this dynamic effect. These children may be helped considerably by receiving instruction on quiet slow breathing techniques at times when they are well, rather in the same way that breathing patterns are taught in an antenatal class. The child can then adopt this more efficient breathing pattern in subsequent attacks. This often provides a considerable increase in the child's confidence in coping with an attack, and may well reduce the tendency to panic.

Chest wall deformity   Chest wall deformity results from two separate mechanisms. These are overinflation of the lungs secondary to small-airways obstruction, and distortion due to increased diaphragmatic muscle activity (Harrison sulci, see Figure 7.2). Both these mechanisms will be overcome if the underlying asthma control is improved. It is difficult to see how physiotherapy can have any role to play in this situation, other than to increase the child's confidence.

PSYCHOTHERAPY

The magnitude of the placebo reaction in asthmatic children has sometimes been taken as an indication that asthmatic children tend to be neurotic. Those who believe this often tell parents that their children should 'pull themselves together' and are reluctant to prescribe appropriate antiasthma drug therapy. It is important to stress that careful control studies have failed to support the contention that asthmatic children are more neurotic than their unaffected peers.[2] On the other hand, it is also important to recognize that acute severe asthma is very frightening; on occasions imminent death seems a very real threat to parents and children alike. The anxiety associated with acute breathlessness is counterproductive, as it tends to increase dynamic compression during expiration. Asthma attacks are also more common and often more severe at times of stress, for example in the days and weeks before crucial exams—a phenomenon common to most chronic illnesses throughout life. For this reason it is important that those caring for children with asthma are sensitive to signs of emotional stress, at home or at school, which may be contributing to the severity of the child's symptoms.

There are many reasons for a child's asthma control to deteriorate, including recent respiratory tract infection and increased allergen exposure. Where the factor responsible is not obvious, time should be set aside to allow the child and his parents to express their worries and to explore the possibility that there may be relationship problems between the parents, between parents and the child, or perhaps involving grandparents. Equally, asthma control often deteriorates when the child has difficulty relating to a new teacher or cannot cope with the academic demands made on him. Occasionally circumstances will be identified which require expert help at child guidance clinics or which may need referral to family therapy units.

HUMIDITY

Parents often request information on the role of humidity. On the one hand, those who live in damp conditions may request letters supporting transfer to dry accommodation; on the other hand, those with dry, centrally heated bedrooms want to know whether they should be buying humidifiers. As with so many other aspects of asthma control, our information is limited. There are no studies indicating that damp conditions lead to

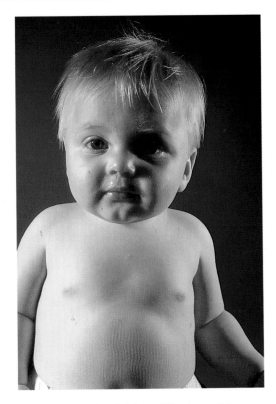

Figure 7.2 A child with bilateral Harrison sulci.

worse asthma control, although high humidity will encourage fungal growth and will help proliferation of house dust mite, and both these factors can reasonably be considered to be adverse. Very dry air may contribute to nocturnal symptoms by drying the secretions within the airways. This is more likely to occur if the child has nasal obstructions and needs to breathe through the mouth. On balance it is probably reasonable to support parents in their efforts to transfer away from very damp conditions and to advise those with central heating to reduce the bedroom temperature to moderate levels (10–15°C/50–60°F) and so save on heating bills, rather than spend money on relatively inefficient and yet quite expensive humidifying devices.

HOUSING

Parents whose children have troublesome asthma often seek advice on the importance of local environmental factors, and may be prepared and financially able to move to another house locally or to another part of the country. Some even raise the possibility of moving to other parts of the world. This is a difficult area for the doctor, as it is rarely possible to quantify the importance of different environmental factors. It would seem reasonable for children with severe hay fever symptoms not to live in the country surrounded by fields, but it is important to remember that winds carry pollens for long distances, so that even those living in the largest and most plant-barren of cities may still have troublesome hay fever symptoms. It would seem equally reasonable to avoid industrial areas where air pollution is high, but again there can be no guarantee that the child's asthma will be appreciably different on moving to other parts of the country. Parents quite often find that their child's asthma does improve after a house move, but this is by no means universal and may be only temporary. For this reason it is unwise to encourage parents to uproot their child from friends at school and spend a considerable amount of money on the assumption that the end result will be significantly better.

HOLIDAYS

Although holidays should be a time for all members of the family to relax and recharge their batteries, those with asthmatic children sometimes view the prospect with considerable anxiety; what should be a pleasurable experience may be marred by a deterioration in the child's asthma, leading either to a curtailment of the holiday or even admission to a strange hospital. Although deterioration in a child's asthma is sometimes unpredictable and therefore unavoidable, the family should be encouraged to take a number of simple steps to reduce the risk that the holiday will be spoilt:

- Parents must ensure that the child has a sufficient supply of drugs for the holiday period
- Parents must be aware of the names of the drugs and the strength of the preparations the child is receiving, so that replacements can be obtained if necessary.

If the child has a relatively severe attack of asthma, he may well be unable to use his standard inhaler device and so alternative delivery systems should be immediately available:

- The 'coffee-cup' system (see page 50)
- A foot-pump nebulizer device (see Figure 7.3) which can be used where there is no regular electricity supply.

If the child is on regular nebulization therapy, the family should ensure that a suitable mains electricity supply is available or that the compressor can be operated from a car battery. Those children who require short courses of systemic steroids for deterioration in their asthma obviously need at least one, and preferably two, complete courses to cover the holiday period.

It is difficult to advise what type of holiday is likely to suit a particular child. Fortunately, parents usually manage to find which environment suits the child best, whether this be a seaside holiday or a visit to another country. Parents should also be advised to obtain the telephone number of a local family practitioner as soon as they arrive at their holiday location, and to check the geographical location of the nearest hospital with accident and emergency facilities. It is important to remind them that not

Figure 7.3 A foot pump nebulizer system, particularly useful for journeys and holidays.

all accident and emergency departments are open every night and weekend, as these are the very times when emergency help is most likely to be needed.

ROLE OF SPECIAL SCHOOLS

In the past many children with severe asthma were transferred to 'special outdoor' schools, on the assumption that they had 'weak chests' and had difficulty coping with the rigours of normal school life. Some were sent to live at relatively high altitudes, where the air was considered to be purer. Many children showed an improvement, perhaps in part due to the relative absence of the house dust mite in mountainous areas. This fashion has disappeared largely due to the introduction of new drugs which have helped to ease management problems.

There remain a small number of children who have severe asthma which is very resistant to therapy on an outpatient or clinic basis but who show rapid improvement in a hospital environment. It is obviously important for the child's home to be visited, as there may be an important allergen which has been overlooked by the parents. It will also be necessary to explore the possibility that the child's symptoms are not related to excessive emotional stress (see page 80). If these exercises prove fruitless and the child needs frequent hospital admissions despite regular systemic steroid therapy, residential schools should be considered and the child referred on a trial basis. It is obviously necessary to ensure that the residential school has first-class medical cover, preferably with a resident nurse, as children with such severe asthma may deteriorate rapidly, possibly with fatal results.

PRACTICAL POINTS

- Physiotherapy has a role when secretions are blocking airways. Breathing exercises may help children who tend to panic during attacks. They do not strengthen respiratory muscles or reduce chest wall deformity.

- Physiotherapy or family counselling is indicated when emotional factors are contributing significantly to the child's symptoms.

- Humidifiers are rarely, if ever, indicated.

- Damp, mould-infested houses are on balance bad for children with troublesome asthma.

- Holidays should be planned with care.

- Special schools are needed only for a very small number of children with severe symptoms who require frequent hospital admissions.

8
Alternative therapies

Even though conventional therapy is so effective for the majority of asthmatic children, some parents are still wary about the use of 'drugs' and would rather turn to what they may consider to be more natural, and so safer, forms of therapy. These include herbal drugs, homeopathy, acupuncture, yoga, negative-ion generators and hypnosis.

HERBAL REMEDIES

There are many herbal 'cures' for asthma (see Table 8.1). A number of these have been shown to have bronchodilator properties, and indeed some of our current preparations are derived from or based on extracts from herbs. Eighteenth and nineteenth century doctors recommended the use of strong coffee or tea (caffeine being a drug closely related to theophylline), stramonium or squill (alkaloids with anticholinergic properties), and if necessary, opium. Opium and its derivatives morphine and heroin are now strongly contraindicated in the management of asthma because they are respiratory depressants, but they can be very effective, presumably due to their actions on the central nervous system rather than any local effects in the lungs. Stramonium, which was often inhaled as cigarette smoke, is also considered to be too toxic for general use. The evidence that other, less toxic, preparations have more than a mild placebo action is unproven, but they are usually safe and parents can be reassured on this point if they wish to explore the use of a particular preparation. The only caveat is that some preparations which have been marketed have high concentrations of systemic steroids. These should obviously be avoided.

Table 8.1 Herbal asthma 'cures'

Ammonicum*	Coltsfoot	Hyssop
Anise	Comfrey	Juniper berry
Boneset	Eucalyptus*	Larkspur
Butterbur	Fig*	Lobelia
Camphor	Garlic	Masterwort
Cherry laurel	Honeysuckle	Passion flower
Coffee	Hore hound	Red rout
		Sesame

*Inhaled as mist. All others taken by mouth.

HOMEOPATHY

Homeopathy was introduced about two hundred years ago largely as a result of the teachings of Samuel Hahnemann, and now has widespread support. It is based on the theory that symptoms can be relieved by giving minute quantities of drugs or chemicals which in large doses would produce those same symptoms. Thus minute doses of arsenic are given for abdominal pain. It is claimed that the curative effect is directly related to the extent of the dilution. Homeopathy has been used for many years in the treatment of asthma, and there are now a number of recommended drugs generally available from herbal stores and shops (see Table 8.2). Parents keen to try this form of therapy can again be reassured that, as the quantity of a drug or chemical is so small, there can be no side-effects. Again, there are no control trials to support the suggestion that these preparations act in any other way than by placebo mechanisms.

Table 8.2 Homeopathic asthma 'cures'

Arsenicum album
Cacarea phosphorica
Hepar sulphuris
Ipecacuana
Kali carbonicum
Phosphorus
Psorinum
Pulsatilla

ACUPUNCTURE

Acupuncture has received increasing interest as a treatment of asthma in recent years. This traditional Chinese therapy is based on the hypothesis that in health there is a balanced flow of energy along twenty-six main circuits or lines which cover the body. This flow becomes unbalanced during illness. Balanced flow can be restored by inserting needles into specific points along the meridia, depending on the organ involved. The needles must be inserted into the subcutaneous tissues and remain there for up to several minutes, and are said to induce a sensation of local warmth. Our information on the place of acupuncture in childhood asthma is very limited. One study in adult asthmatic patients failed to find any difference if the needles were inserted in the traditional places or at random.[1] Interestingly, both groups showed significant short-term improvement.

YOGA

Although yoga has been used mildly in the management of adult asthma, it may be of use for adolescent children because it teaches them to relax.[2] The yoga regime adopted usually involves several rhythmic breathing techniques combined with simple hand and body movements, yoga exercises to loosen joints, maintenance of a physical posture and meditation. It is claimed that yoga may stabilize and reduce the excitability of the nervous system, and thus significantly reduce the level of anxiety.

NEGATIVE-ION GENERATORS

Negative-ion generators are widely marketed. Information supporting their use rests mainly on the finding that high positive-ion concentrations in the air lead to a degree of airways obstruction in laboratory rats.[3] Further support is provided by anecdotal findings that asthma tends to be worse during thunderstorms, when the positive-ion concentration rises. There have been two papers providing more rigorous evidence. One showed that a high positive-ion concentration tended to increase airways lability, the other that negative ions tended to have the opposite effect. Studies have so far failed to show that asthma control is improved by actually having such a device running in the home. Although this is an interesting area, there is insufficient evidence to recommend that these devices should be purchased for domestic use.

HYPNOSIS

Hypnosis has also been used in an attempt to reduce the severity of asthma symptoms. The aim is not to convince the child that he does not have asthma, but rather to teach him methods of autosuggestion which can then be used when asthma symptoms commence. This form of therapy has not lived up to expectations, and it is used relatively infrequently. This is partly a reaction to the worry that autosuggestion might reduce the child's perception of the severity of an attack, rather than affect the attack itself. This could be very dangerous, as it would discourage the child and his parents from seeking additional help at times when airways obstruction is getting progressively worse, despite therapy. There are a small group of children who panic as soon as they feel asthma symptoms starting. For these patients hypnosis should certainly be considered if instruction on simple breathing techniques fails to improve their confidence and reduce anxiety.

PRACTICAL POINTS

- Herbal remedies are used quite extensively. Some have weak bronchodilator properties. Parents should be advised that some contain high doses of systemic steroids.

- The role of homeopathy remains unproven.

- Acupuncture and yoga may have a useful place for some, although there is no controlled evidence for their role in childhood asthma.

- Negative-ion generators have mild beneficial physiological effects but these do not justify their use clinically.

- Hypnosis remains controversial.

9
Specific asthma problems

Many asthmatic children have specific asthma problems which respond well to modifications to standard antiasthma therapy.

It has been known since the mid 1960s that prolonged stressful exercise produces an initial bronchodilatation followed by bronchoconstriction coming on usually 6–10min after the onset of the exercise.[1] This pattern of response probably affects all asthmatic children at some time or other. The response is more likely to be positive if the child has a cold or has had recent exposure to an allergen to which he is sensitive, for example, in the hay fever season. This exercise response is irritating to many asthmatics, frustrating to those who have athletic ambitions and devastating to a small group of highly sensitive children who can become cyanosed within a few minutes of starting to run. It is extremely important to take a very positive approach to ensure that even relatively severe EIB does not prevent the child from taking part in play and game activities, as this will tend to isolate him from his non-asthmatic peers.

Type of exercise

As EIB is brought on by inhaling dry air, children find that running outdoors in cold weather provides the worse possible conditions. Conversely, exercising in relatively enclosed areas, such as squash courts, is more favourable. The best exercising conditions are often provided by a heated indoor swimming pool where the air over the water is not only warm but highly humidified. Unfortunately, a small number of asthmatic children react to the chlorine used to purify the water. This tends to negate the advantages.

Use of refractory period

Although the mechanism remains obscure, repeated exercise challenge produces less bronchoconstriction, ie, there is a refractory period lasting for up to 1 hour (see Figure 9.1). Brief, strenuous exercise, up to 2min, usually induces some degree of bronchodilatation without subsequent bronchoconstriction. Fortunately this brief exercise is also sufficient to induce the refractory effects, so that three or four brief runs taking between 1 and 2 min each over a 10–15 min period will often allow the child to take part in prolonged stress with fewer, if any, asthma symptoms.[2]

Training programmes

There are now a number of studies showing that intensive exercise training programmes help children to take part in physical activities that were previously not open to them. These training sessions are often run by physiotherapists at local swimming pools, taking advantage of the warm, humid conditions. A number of children find a new confidence as a result of participation in these programmes which also make full use of drug therapy and the refractory period.[3] Current information suggests that the exercises do not have a direct effect on the airways themselves but act by increasing the child's fitness, so that more can be undertaken before critical levels of hyperventilation and airways drying are exceeded.

Drug therapy

Inhaled beta$_2$ stimulants provide a most effective method for blocking EIB. The stimulant is equally effective if inhaled as an aerosol or taken as a powder and is usually effective for up to 2 hours (see Figure 9.2). This blocking effect represents a true prophylactic effect rather than merely increasing airways calibre, so that any bronchoconstrictor effect is less apparent.[4] Oral beta$_2$ stimulants also have similar actions but need to be given in massive doses, which will then presumably produce similar concentrations in the airways.[5] Almost all children can cope with even the most competitive aims using their beta$_2$ stimulant inhalers. Others find that prolonged runs still produce breakthrough coughing and wheezing. A few, less than 5 per cent, still have troublesome symptoms which limit their ability to join in with even relatively short bursts of exercise.

Inhaled sodium cromoglycate is also an effective EIB blocking agent with a similar duration of action to the beta$_2$ stimulants.[6] There are, however, rather more asthmatic children (30 per cent) who fail to obtain significant relief. The mechanism by which the sodium cromoglycate works is unknown. Some children who are on regular sodium cromoglycate therapy get such good prophylactic benefit that they do not even need to use their beta$_2$ stimulants before heavy physical activity.

Theophyllines and ipratropium bromide have more variable and less impressive EIB blocking characteristics. They do not provide useful alternative therapy.[7]

Topical and systemic steroids are interesting as they appear to be ineffective if given as single doses in the hour before an exercise challenge, but do modify the response if taken regularly for at least two to three weeks.[8] This probably represents the ability of the steroids to alter airways lability when taken over a period of weeks. There is certainly a significant number of asthmatic children who find that EIB ceases to be a problem once they receive topical steroids on a regular morning and evening basis.

The practical approach is to encourage children to inhale beta$_2$ stimulants in the minutes before commencing games, taking two to three puffs from their aerosol or an equivalent dose of beta$_2$ stimulant powder. If this fails, commence the child on regular sodium cromoglycate therapy with additional doses or, if necessary, beta$_2$ stimulants immediately before games. If this too is ineffective, change over to twice daily topical steroids with additional doses of beta$_2$ stimulants immediately before games.

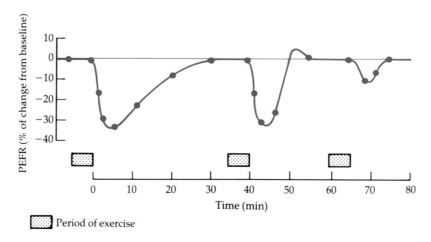

Period of exercise

Figure 9.1 The fall in peak flow on exercise drops progressively with repeated tests.

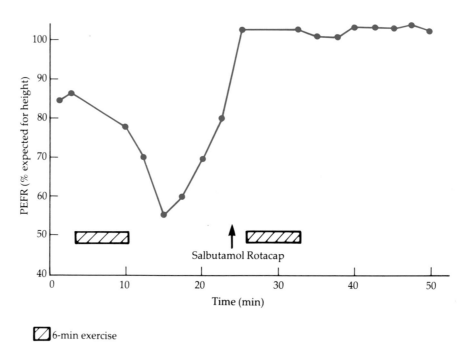

6-min exercise

Figure 9.2 The fall in peak flow after a 6-min exercise is totally blocked by the prior inhalation of salbutamol.

NOCTURNAL ASTHMA

Asthma symptoms are often most troublesome at night, particularly between 2am and 4am or on waking in the morning. There are several different mechanisms which could be responsible for this nocturnal deterioration (see Table 9.1) but at present we have little information on their relative contributions.[9]

Table 9.1 Factors responsible for nocturnal asthma

House dust mite
Low plasma cortisol
Diurnal variations in airways calibre
Low environmental temperatures
Mouth breathing
Duration of drug therapy

House dust mite

House dust mite population is greatest within the child's bed, as its main food source is shed human skin scales. It is obvious that exposure to this potential allergen will be greatest during the night. The relatively poor response to house dust mite avoidance measures suggests that this may be of limited importance.

Steroid secretion

The endogenous corticosteroid release falls to a minimum in the early hours of the night.

Diurnal variations

Throughout life there are diurnal variations in airways calibres with peak bronchodilatation mid-afternoon and peak bronchoconstriction in the early hours. This diurnal variation is more obvious in asthmatic patients but its mechanism is unknown. Studies on adults have suggested that it is independent of the corticosteroid secretion pattern.

Air temperature

Many asthmatic children breathe through the mouth at night, as they often have associated nasal pathology. Inhaling cold and relatively dry air may induce bronchoconstriction.

Duration of drug action

Standard beta$_2$ stimulant, theophylline and sodium cromoglycate preparations all have relatively short durations of action, lasting up to 6 hours. Inevitably efficacy will drop as the night proceeds so that there will often be little, if any, drug action by 2–3am.

Management

Although there are a number of slow-release beta$_2$ stimulant preparations on the market, control studies have indicated that they have a limited place in the management of nocturnal asthma and early morning dipping. Part of this may be due to the formulations available. Slow-release theophyllines have proved to be superior[10] and the treatment of choice is a single slow-release (8–12 hours) tablet or capsule on going to bed in the evening. Those too young to swallow capsules can take the contents as minipellets from a teaspoon. This single-dose therapy rarely produces any nausea or vomiting, but may cause bedwetting secondary to the diuretic effect. Those who continue to have troublesome symptoms can often be helped by taking inhaled topical steroids on a morning and evening basis—if necessary with slow-release theophyllines.

COLLAPSE OF SEGMENTS OR LOBES

Sometimes deterioration in asthma symptoms is associated with, if not due to, persisting collapse of the segment or lobe, often the right middle lobe. This is presumably secondary to thick secretions which have blocked off the lumen. If the collapse persists, secondary infective changes may occur which will prevent re-expansion and/or lead to localized bronchiectasis. The presence of the collapse is noted usually on chest x-ray only and it is then often impossible to determine how long it has been present.

These children should be given nebulized beta$_2$ stimulants two or three times a day and should also receive intensive physiotherapy from the local physiotherapist and also from their parents. Chest x-ray should be repeated after one to two weeks. If there is no improvement, the child needs to be admitted to hospital and have bronchial toilet carried out at bronchoscopy. It is certainly worth trying to inflate the affected lobe while the child is under an anaesthetic and, if this fails, to repeat the chest x-ray after injecting a radio-opaque dye into the affected area in order to visualize the extent of the damage. Under these circumstances it will be necessary to assess the extent to which the collapse is contributing to the child's symptoms and whether a lobectomy is needed. This is a difficult decision, but not normally an urgent one. Collapse of the upper lobes is less likely to produce longterm problems than collapse of the lower or right middle lobes, which tend to accumulate secretions and then become chronically infected.

BRONCHIECTASIS AND ASTHMA

A small number of children have asthma as defined by strikingly abnormal airways lability and good symptom relief with antiasthma therapy, but who also cough up offensive green sputum at least once a day. In some, the green appearance is due to an excess of eosinophils; these children have a form of Loeffler's syndrome. In others, the sputum contains an excess of neutrophils and will often grow pathogens, such as *Haemophilus influenzae*, pneumococci, klebsiella, pseudomonas or even *Staphylococcus aureus*. In these patients, the chest x-ray will often show cystic shadows in the lower zones, indicating that the child has bronchiectasis. This may be due to an immune or ciliary abnormality (see Table 9.2). Others have a non-progressive abnormality, due either to a persisting collapse or to a destructive infective illness earlier in childhood.

It is not always possible to ascertain whether the asthma is purely a secondary response to chronic inflammatory airways damage, whether the bronchiectasis is due to asthma complications earlier in childhood, or whether the child has acquired asthma and bronchiectasis independently.

Table 9.2 Causes of bronchiectasis

Slowly resolving pneumonia
Cystic fibrosis
Immotile cilia syndrome
Hypogammaglobulinaemia
Neutrophil defects
Measles

Management

These children obviously require treatment for both bronchiectasis and asthma. They will require postural drainage, percussion, and probably forced expiratory breathing morning and night to aid bronchial drainage. They will also need prior treatment with inhaled bronchodilator drugs, preferably using a nebulizer/compressor system to overcome any tendency to bronchoconstrict during the procedure and to improve lung clearance. Antibiotic therapy will be required at times when the child is febrile and unwell. Sputum should be sent off for culture at each clinic appointment and whenever the child is unwell, so that the bacterial pathogen responsible can be identified and antibiotic treatment modified.

Most of these children will require additional prophylactic asthma therapy. For this, twice daily topical steroids, inhaled as an aerosol or as a powder, are more likely to be effective than sodium cromoglycate. There is a theoretical risk that the combination of topical steroids and antibiotics might lead to severe pulmonary fungal infection, but in practice this does not seem to occur. The child will also need to have ready access to inhaled beta$_2$ stimulants for breakthrough attacks of wheezing and coughing during the day.

PRACTICAL POINTS

- EIB is a common problem in childhood asthma. Most patients can be helped by prior treatment with inhaled beta$_2$ stimulants or sodium cromoglycate.

- Swimming is a particularly useful form of exercise.

- Training programmes will increase a child's confidence and delay the onset of symptoms because of improved fitness.

- Nocturnal asthma is common, and usually responds well to slow-release theophylline preparations.

- Collapse of a lung segment or lobe requires intensive therapy with inhaled beta$_2$ stimulants and physiotherapy. Sometimes surgery is required.

- Bronchiectasis is a rare but important associated condition.

10
Management of an acute asthma attack

DIFFERENTIAL DIAGNOSIS

Most families whose child is admitted to hospital with acute airways obstruction will already know that their child has asthma. For a few it will be the first severe attack, or even an isolated event. Throughout childhood, asthma is by far the commonest cause of acute airways obstruction but other conditions need to be considered. In the first year of life, the next most frequent condition is acute bronchiolitis. The main differentiating features of bronchiolitis are the predominance of fine crepitations throughout the lung fields with striking hyperinflation, sometimes but not always accompanied by wheezing. Other conditions which can usually be differentiated by careful history, examination and chest x-ray are heart failure, milk aspiration and congenital lobar emphysema (see Table 10.1).

Table 10.1 Differential diagnosis of asthma in infancy

Acute bronchiolitis
Pneumonia
Heart failure
Recurrent aspiration
H type tracheo-oesophageal fistula
Congenital lobar emphysema
Bronchopulmonary dysplasia
Bronchomalacia

Between the ages of one and five years, the chances that any wheezing attack is due to asthma increases further, although acute bronchiolitis does occur in this age group, and toddlers not infrequently inhale solid objects, including peanuts, small toys and even springs (see Figure 10.1). Sometimes acute laryngotracheobronchitis (croup) is confused with asthma. With care and an open mind, it should not be difficult to appreciate that the child has a predominant inspiratory stridor, even if there are associated expiratory stridor and even rhonchi on expiration.

In schoolchildren, the association between an acute attack of wheezing and the diagnosis of asthma becomes even closer. Bronchiolitis is now rare, although adenoviral infections do occur and can cause devastating and persisting obstructive airways disease. A spontaneous pneumothorax will produce acute breathlessness and wheezing but is relatively easy to diagnose as air entry will be considerably reduced on the affected side; chest x-ray is almost always diagnostic. Bronchial foreign bodies can sometimes produce a ball-valve obstruction with breathlessness and wheezing. Chest x-rays on inspiration and expiration will usually reveal that the affected lobe fails to deflate on expiration (see Figure 10.2). If necessary this can be confirmed by gamma camera ventilation/perfusion studies, and the offending object removed at bronchoscopy. Hysterical hyperventilation is sometimes mistaken for asthma, although the affected children, usually adolescent girls, are not hyperinflated and do not as a rule have any wheezing symptoms.

Identification of trigger factors

Sometimes the trigger responsible for the admission is relatively easy to identify. The majority of asthma attacks needing hospital treatment are due to viral infections. For example, the number of children admitted to hospital rises dramatically during the annual RSV epidemic. Other causes include prolonged exposure to high pollen or high fungal spore concentrations, producing an increase in admission in the spring and autumn respectively. Food allergens are rarely implicated, but emotional factors may be important to some children.

Initial clinical assessment

History   The most important facts to obtain from the parents are:

- How has the child responded to therapy in previous attacks
- What regular therapy is the child receiving (particularly steroids or theophylline)
- What therapy has already been given?

Clinical examination should:

- Provide an invaluable baseline
- Help to determine the therapy that the child requires
- Enable the child's progress and response to drugs to be measured.

Appearance   It can be difficult to recognize even quite severe cyanosis in artificial light. If there is any doubt, give the child oxygen by face mask and see if this produces a noticeable colour change. Sometimes the hypoxia produces pallor, anxiety and restlessness, rather than obvious cyanosis. Again, if there is any doubt give the child oxygen. It is also essential to document the child's mental state. Most will be very anxious; some will be very tired and perhaps rapidly reaching a state of exhaustion when they may be unable to maintain adequate ventilation. Very occasionally, the attack is so severe that the child will be unconscious and, on superficial examination, the gravity of the situation may be underestimated. It is essential to enquire whether the child has been given a sedative, as this can contribute to the picture and to the problems.

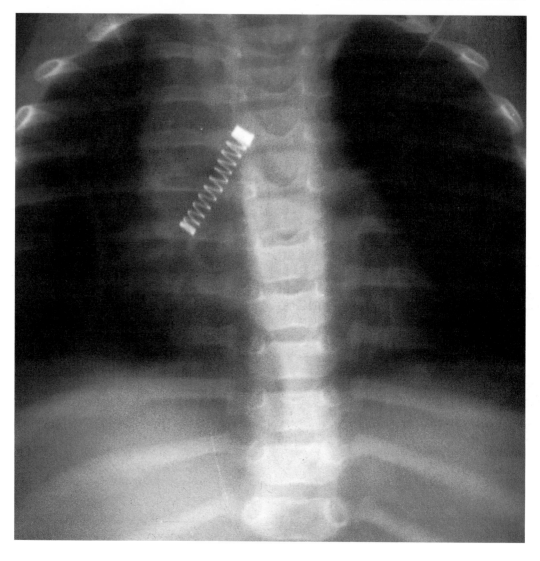

Figure 10.1 An inhaled spring causing wheezing in a three-year-old child; seen on x-ray.

Heart rate   Severe asthma is invariably associated with tachycardia, with rates in excess of 130/min. Unfortunately tachycardia may also be the result of therapy, as all bronchodilator drugs will produce an increase in heart rate. Aminophylline is particularly prone to do this. It is well worth pressing gently on a radial artery with an index finger until the pulse virtually disappears distally. This can be felt with the middle finger. A fluctuation in pulse pressure in phase with respiration indicates that the child has a significant degree of pulsus paradoxus, which can be documented in the standard

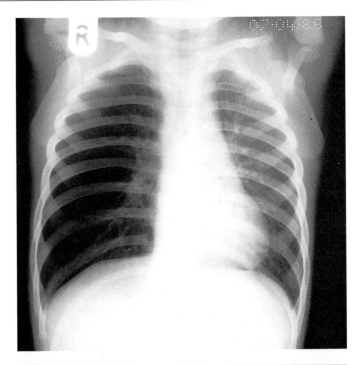

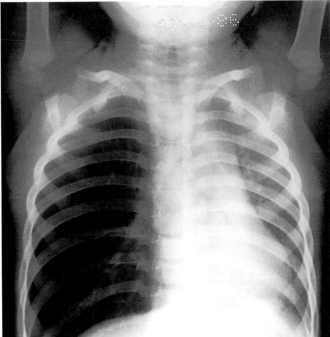

Figure 10.2 Inspiratory and expiratory films of a child who had been treated for asthma for six months. Careful testing revealed that there was a sudden onset of symptoms in a previously well child. The 'asthma' resolved when the peanut was removed from the right main bronchus.

way with a sphygmomanometer and stethoscope. A pulsus paradoxus of more than 20 mmHg confirms that the child is producing very large intrathoracic pressure swings and has severe airways obstruction.[2]

Respiratory pattern   Respiratory rates also increase during asthma attacks, with a tendency for the inspiratory/expiratory rate ratio to be reduced. Babies and young children are more likely to breathe at higher rates than physiologists would recommend from their knowledge of the time constant of the lung in asthma!

Careful visual examination of the child's chest and abdomen can provide far more information on the severity of the asthma than even the most thorough auscultatory exercise:

- First decide whether the child is hyperinflated. Are the child's shoulders in an elevated position? Does the upper part of his chest protrude? When viewed from the side, is the anterior/posterior diameter of the child's chest increased?
- Second, look for evidence that the accessory respiratory muscles have been recruited. For this it is particularly useful to look carefully at the child's abdominal wall, as this will indicate the extent to which the child is using his abdominal muscles to help force air out against the airways obstruction.
- Finally, document the extent to which the tissues in the suprasternal and intercostal spaces recess on inspiration, as this will provide further information on the pressures generated within the thorax.

Palpation and percussion   It is important to check that the trachea is central and that the cardiac impulse has not been displaced, as the child may have a pneumothorax or have collapse of one or more lobes. It is also well worth examining the abdomen to note the extent to which the liver has been displaced by the hyperinflation of the lungs.

Percussion is not particularly helpful. It may be that the area of cardiac dullness is reduced, but this is a relatively inefficient method for assessing hyperinflation. Percussion certainly helps identify the lower border of the liver, as this is not always easy to feel when the child's abdominal muscles are contracting.

Auscultation   The relationship between auscultatory findings and severity of asthma is poor, as rhonchi will only be heard if air flow is turbulent in the larger airways. If there is extensive small-airways obstruction, the child may be unable to generate a sufficiently high flow to produce much noise. For this reason, a relatively quiet chest in the presence of other visual signs of airways obstruction suggests that the asthma is severe. Reduction in breath sounds over one lung suggests either that there has been plugging of large airways and collapse, or that there is a pneumothorax on that side. This problem can usually be resolved by comparing the percussion note over both sides of the chest and looking for evidence of mediastinal shift towards or away from the affected side. Many children will have coarse crepitations in addition to rhonchi, due to secretions within the airways. This does not necessarily mean that they have a bacterial infection and require antibiotics.

Figure 10.3 A child blowing into a peak flow meter, useful for clinic and home monitoring.

Initial investigations

Lung function tests   Where possible, measure the degree of airways obstruction with a peak flow meter. This will produce a more objective measurement by which to monitor progress, but is not possible in children under the age of five or six years. Even some older children are too disturbed to cooperate satisfactorily (see Figure 10.3). A peak flow measurement of less than 20 per cent of that expected for height indicates very severe asthma; values between 20 per cent and 40 per cent indicate moderately severe asthma.

Chest x-ray   The large majority of chest x-rays taken during the acute phase of an asthma attack show only hyperinflation and sometimes linear streaks, due to mild linear collapse. Therefore, chest x-rays should only be taken for three reasons: if there is doubt about the diagnosis, if clinical examination suggests that the child may have either lobar collapse or pneumothorax, or if response to the therapy is abnormally slow.

Arterial blood gases   Although arterial blood gases can provide information on the progress of the asthma attack, these need not be tested unless the child is obviously cyanosed, is not normally alert, or is failing to respond to therapy. If necessary, arterial blood can be obtained from radial or brachial arteries, after injection of local anaesthetic.

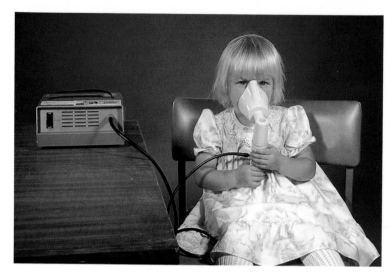

Figure 10.4 The nebulizer compressor system provides the best means for ensuring that beta$_2$ stimulants penetrate deep into the airways.

Initial therapy

The first line of treatment for acute severe asthma is to provide the child with inhaled beta$_2$ stimulants. This can best be given using a nebulizer/compressor system, which is as effective as intravenous therapy and produces less tachycardia (see Figure 10.4). If the nebulizer is not immediately available, the child can use his standard inhaler device, whether this be an aerosol (three puffs) or a Rotahaler (400 µg). If the airways obstruction is severe and limits inspiratory flow to such an extent that delivery is severely impaired, use either the coffee-cup delivery system or an interface unit, such as the Nebuhaler or Aerochamber. Inhaled beta$_2$ stimulants should be given even if the child has received this form of treatment several times at home without improvement, because the environment has now changed and the inhaled dose is so small that no harm can come to the child.

Two to three min after the end of the inhalation, reassess the degree of airways obstruction clinically and where possible by the peak flow measurement. There are then three possible lines of action:

- The child improves dramatically. In this case, he should be observed for an hour. If improvement is maintained he can then return home with instructions to repeat his inhalations every 3–4 hours, but return if the asthma once more slips out of control.
- The child shows definite improvement but continues to have signs of hyperinflation and increased work of breathing. In this situation, he needs to be admitted to the ward for observation and will require a minimum of nebulized stimulants every 2–4 hours.
- The child shows no response to nebulized beta$_2$ stimulants and continues to have signs of severe airways obstruction. In this situation, he should be given intravenous aminophylline while the heart rate is monitored with an

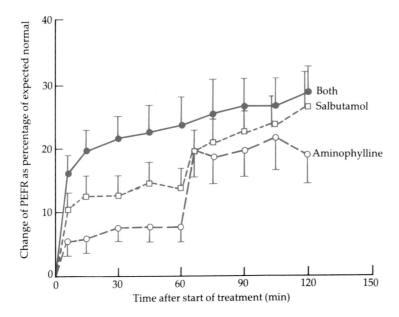

Figure 10.5 The effect of nebulized salbutamol (□), intravenous aminophylline (○) and both combined (●) on the peak flow of children in status asthmaticus.

ECG. For those who are not on oral theophylline, a loading dose of 4 mg/kg can be given over 5–10 min. If the child is on regular theophylline therapy, some authorities recommend giving one half of the loading dose, others that the loading dose should be omitted totally. The child should then receive a continuous infusion of 0.7 mg/kg per hour. Although beta$_2$ stimulants and theophyllines are both said to increase intracellular cyclic AMP levels, albeit by different mechanisms, there seem to be some children who benefit from combined therapy (see Figure 10.5). If the child shows an improvement within 15–20 min, he can be transferred to the ward for continuous intravenous aminophylline therapy with inhaled beta$_2$ stimulants every 2–3 hours. A patient who does not show any improvement should be commenced on intravenous hydrocortisone (100–200 mg) and admitted to an area where he can be monitored intensively.

Inpatient management

All children admitted to the ward require recordings of heart rate, respiratory rate, level of consciousness and, where applicable, peak flow four-hourly as a minimum, until they are obviously well on the way to recovery and peak flows have risen to 60 per cent of the expected value. Continuous ECG monitoring is essential if the child is also receiving intravenous aminophylline.

Those children who have failed to show any improvement and have been put on intravenous hydrocortisone need hourly nursing observations (heart rate, respiratory rate and general condition) and also need a chest x-ray and arterial blood gas. The blood gases should be tested every 4–6 hours until the child shows signs of improvement.

ADDITIONAL THERAPY

Ipratropium bromide may be of benefit to some children who respond poorly to beta$_2$ stimulants and aminophylline. One study found that ipratropium bromide produced a useful improvement when lung function plateaued on nebulized salbutamol.[3] Other studies have been less encouraging, however, finding that a combination of ipratropium bromide and salbutamol had no advantage over salbutamol alone.

Sedatives have no place in the management of acute severe asthma. They have in the past been given to children who are very anxious. Sedatives are not only dangerous, but may paradoxically increase the child's distress by making him more confused. In fact a child usually responds to confident reassurance from his parents and the medical and nursing team. Sometimes hypoxia may contribute to the child's distress: if this is suspected, the child should be given supplementary oxygen.

Oxygen therapy

As described on page 95, hypoxia occurs earlier in asthma, due to ventilation/perfusion mismatching. For this reason, oxygen therapy sometimes has an important role in the management of acute severe asthma.

Modes of administration

Nebulizers work equally well whether driven by air or 100 per cent oxygen. In the ward, and in the accident and emergency department, it is often preferable to use oxygen from either a cylinder or a wall supply. This will relieve any hypoxia during the period of administration. There is also the theoretical advantage that it will overcome any transitory drop in arterial tension due to the bronchodilator drugs themselves. It is well known that nebulized isoprenaline tends to make ventilation/perfusion abnormalities worse by increasing blood supply to poorly ventilated units. The evidence that this happens with beta$_2$ selective drugs used in normal therapeutic doses is at present weak, but on the other hand there are no good reasons for not using oxygen in this situation.

Oxygen cannulae provide the most convenient and least threatening delivery system for children (see Figure 10.6). There is no need to restrict the oxygen supply, since the carbon dioxide chemoreceptor drive remains intact, at least until the child is deeply unconscious and the arterial carbon dioxide level is grossly elevated. Usually a flow of 2–3 l/min will be adequate to overcome any hypoxia. For this and other delivery systems, the oxygen should be bubbled through water so that it is at least partially humidified.

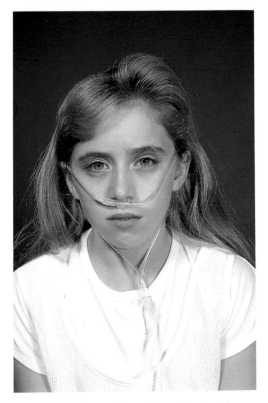

Figure 10.6 Light-weight nasal cannulae for delivering oxygen.

Face masks are preferable for younger children. Parents are usually happy to sit with their child and ensure that the face mask remains in place. Positioning is certainly less critical than with the cannulae (see Figure 10.7).

Oxygen tents and head boxes Very restless children or those under the age of three years must be nursed in an enclosure, either a tent or, if very young, a head box. The main advantage of the head box is that the flow requirement is much lower, and it is relatively easy to maintain high oxygen levels.

Unlike the neonatal situation, it is not essential to monitor the ambient oxygen unless the child is critically ill and requires a particularly high oxygen concentration. Any child who requires oxygen therapy needs at least twice daily arterial blood gas tests to assess progress. Transcutaneous oxygen monitors, although producing useful information on short-term trends, are insufficiently reliable to act as a total substitute for arterial blood samples. The new generation of saturation monitors, which are much less sensitive to variations in skin blood flow and largely unaffected by the thickness of the skin, may be more useful.

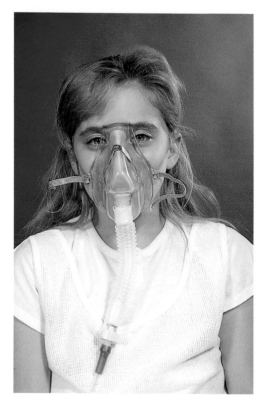

Figure 10.7 An oxygen mask suitable for young children. The concentration is determined by the rate of flow and the connecting insert (coloured yellow).

Physiotherapy

Although airway plugging is a common feature in acute severe asthma, physiotherapy does not usually have a major role to play. These children are often near total exhaustion, and tolerate it poorly. Physiotherapy is of value in situations where plugging has led to widespread collapse. It should always be preceded by nebulized beta$_2$ stimulants.

Hydration and mist therapy

Children admitted to the ward with asthma are often mildly dehydrated. Their respiratory water loss will have increased and many reduce their fluid intake, concentrating all their energies on breathing. This dehydration will tend to thicken airway secretions, leading to airways obstruction locally and collapse distally. In the past, children have often been nursed in mist tents in an attempt to overcome this. It usually involved a venturi jet system which developed a cold mist. Although this produced a dense fog when discharging into a tent around the child, the temperature of the air was relatively low and the water content rarely exceeded 20 mg/l, less than half that produced by drawing air through the nose (see Figure 10.8). High water content can

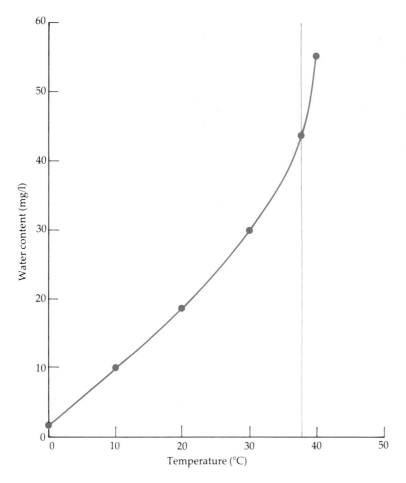

Figure 10.8 The water content of fully saturated air at varying ambient temperatures.

be achieved by using ultrasonic nebulizers (more than 100 mg/l), but this is highly irritant and will induce coughing and make airways obstruction worse. The only alternative is to generate a hot mist. This ensures high water content and is relatively non-irritant but has largely been discontinued as some children have suffered severe burns. A better approach is to encourage the children to take drinks by mouth and to supplement fluids intravenously. Those not responding to beta$_2$ stimulants will already have an intravenous line for aminophylline and if necessary hydrocortisone. This can also be used to provide 4.3 per cent dextrose saline. The optimal fluid intake is not known. One study,[4] measuring intrathoracic pressure, suggested that as airways obstruction increased, the mean intrathoracic pressure tended to fall; that is, the increasingly negative pressures generated were not matched by increasingly positive pressures during expiration. This may, in theory, lead to pulmonary oedema, suggesting that normal maintenance requirements should certainly not be exceeded.

MECHANICAL VENTILATION

Although mechanical ventilation (see Table 10.2) can be life-saving, it is rarely required if standard drug therapy is given appropriately. Respiratory support will usually not be required for status asthmaticus more than once or twice a year, even in units providing care for populations of up to half a million people. The indication for this form of intervention is essentially that the child is not responding to therapy and is on the verge of respiratory arrest. Wherever possible, the decision to ventilate should be an elective one so that the intubation procedure can be carried out by a skilled anaesthetist after inducing anaesthesia. Occasionally, deterioration is too rapid for this; at other times the child is rushed into an accident and emergency department, unconscious and with either feeble or no respiratory efforts. In these circumstances, he must be intubated immediately. For those over eight years of age, a cuffed endotracheal tube is preferable. For children below this age, a straight tube will normally achieve an adequate seal for the high pressures which will be used. Once the endotracheal tube is in place, the child should be ventilated initially using an anaesthetic rebreathing bag with 100 per cent oxygen. The aim must be to achieve reasonable chest wall movement, regardless of inflation pressures needed—these often exceed 40 or even $50\,cmH_2O$. This should be continued until the child is pink and has a stable blood pressure. The mode of fixation at the endotracheal tube will normally be determined by the anaesthetist who may replace the tube used for the initial resuscitation by a nasoendotracheal tube, which many feel is less likely to be displaced.

Table 10.2 Indications for intermittent positive pressure ventilation for acute severe asthma

Respiratory arrest
Coma
Exhaustion

Table 10.3 Causes of rapid deterioration during IPPV

Failure of ventilator
Leak in ventilator circuit
Blocked endotracheal tube
Pneumothorax
Cardiac arrhythmias

Ventilator settings

As the mechanical characteristics of the airways can change rapidly over the first few hours, it is preferable to use a volume-limited time-cycled ventilator, rather than devices which are primarily pressure-limited. Unfortunately the ventilator tidal volume readings will be misleading due to the compliance of the ventilator circuit, so that the volume actually delivered to the child's lungs may be considerably less than those shown. This is a particular problem when the child is relatively small and the circuit relatively large. As a general rule, it is reasonable to provide tidal volumes of 10–20 ml/kg body weight at a rate of 20–30/min with an inspiratory/expiratory ratio of approximately 1:2. On theoretical grounds, positive end-expiratory pressure should be avoided on the grounds that it will increase peak pressure for any given tidal volume, but on occasions it does appear beneficial. Arterial blood gases must be measured 10–20 min after the child has been put on the ventilator so that the settings can be altered appropriately. Full antiasthma drug therapy must obviously be continued. Although some facilities do have nebulization facilities so that the beta$_2$ stimulants can be given directly down the endotracheal tube, it is more usual for the child to be changed on to a continuous infusion of both beta$_2$ stimulant and aminophylline. Systemic steroids (eg, hydrocortisone 2–4 mg/kg) will also be required at 3–4 hourly intervals. Most anaesthetists also prefer to paralyse children requiring ventilatory support for status asthmaticus. This usually involves an initial intravenous dose of pancuronium (0.1 mg/kg) followed by a continuous infusion rate of 0.1 mg/kg per hour. The child will also require drugs to ensure analgesia, sedation and amnesia.

Monitoring during ventilatory support

During the ventilatory period the child will need continuous ECG and respiratory monitoring. As some children become hypotensive, arterial blood pressure should also be measured continuously. Nursing observation will initially need to be carried out every 15 min but this can be reduced to once an hour as soon as the child is reasonably stable.

The pressure required to deliver the set tidal volume also provides very useful information on the child's progress. He will require standard ventilatory nursing care, including 2–4 hourly turning and care to pressure areas, and 2–4 hourly tracheal toilet after instilling 2–10 ml of saline down the endotracheal tube. Blood gas measurements will need to be repeated at 3–4 hourly intervals, or at any time when the child shows signs of deterioration.

The commonest and most worrying reason for sudden deterioration (see Table 10.3) is an air leak. This can very rapidly lead to cardiac arrest.

The paralysis can usually be allowed to wear off once the inflation pressures have fallen to less than 20 cmH$_2$O. This usually occurs within 24–48 hours.

BRONCHIAL LAVAGE

Bronchial lavage has been recommended on the assumption that this will clear secretions and debris from the airways and so reduce airways obstruction. In practice, although the procedure does wash up material, clinical improvement is rarely dramatic. It may be worth trying once the child has been intubated and is relatively stable after a period of manual ventilation (ie, immediately prior to attachment to a ventilator). An injection of 1–2 ml of normal saline/kg body weight is then given down the endotracheal tube and the child manually ventilated up to ten times. The endotracheal tube is then aspirated. This can be repeated several times, provided that the child's condition remains satisfactory and the aspirated fluid shows that secretions are being removed.

THERAPY DURING RECOVERY

Those children who have required intravenous steroids can generally be weaned over to oral preparations (eg, prednisolone 1–2 mg/kg per day) in addition to inhaled beta$_2$

stimulants. It is usually possible to stop intravenous hydrocortisone and aminophylline within 24–48 hours. The oral steroids should be continued for at least five days and then stopped without a period of weaning. Once the child has recovered, his longterm therapy must be reviewed to see whether changes are needed or whether the admission was an isolated and explicable occurrence for a child whose asthma is otherwise well controlled.

PRACTICAL POINTS

- Diagnosis is almost always made on a careful history and examination.

- Document previous therapy and present clinical condition.

- Treat intensively with inhaled beta$_2$ stimulants delivered by nebulizer.

- If that fails, give intravenous aminophylline and if necessary intravenous hydrocortisone.

- Document progress with clinical observation and where possible peak flow.

- Give oxygen early and generously if there is any evidence of hypoxia.

- Supportive ventilation is rarely required.

11
Management of childhood asthma in general practice

Dr Douglas Jenkinson MB ChB FRCGP DObstRCOG DCH

Medicine is full of paradoxes, and the management of children with asthma in general practice is one of them. On the one hand, most asthmatic children can be cared for entirely by the family doctor and, by and large, they respond well to treatment. On the other hand, asthma is underdiagnosed and undertreated in general practice as a whole,[1,2,3] and many asthmatics stay unnecessarily under hospital care. The reasons for this are understandable—they stem from changes in knowledge and attitudes to management over the last two decades that have not been assimilated, and from the large initial investment of time that is required.

Importance of diagnosis

It is fundamentally important to diagnose children with recurrent wheezing as asthmatic,[4] and, for general purposes, a child who wheezes on two separate occasions has asthma. A three-year-old child brought in with mild wheezing with a respiratory infection may not require treatment on that particular occasion, but the parents should be advised to return if there is a further episode of wheezing. On the next visit, the diagnosis of recurrent wheezing, and therefore asthma, can be confirmed.

A diagnosis of bronchitis or wheezy bronchitis will obstruct the provision of specific asthma treatment, since evidence shows that proper treatment depends on a diagnosis of asthma.[5] Those who say that the diagnosis of asthma causes anxiety are merely rationalizing; the evidence is to the contrary.

Making the diagnosis

In order to diagnose asthma at the earliest opportunity, doctors should be particularly suspicious of children who attend frequently with chest problems as many will eventually be diagnosed as asthmatic if it is not clear already.[6] The child's history will usually provide more useful information than an examination, and the diagnosis can strongly be suspected from the history even if the child is well at the time. Again, the opportunity could be taken to instruct the parents to bring the child along the next time he wheezes so that the diagnosis can be confirmed by looking at and listening to the chest for signs of airways obstruction. Sometimes it is useful to demonstrate wheezing by asking the child to run up and down a corridor until puffed. This will commonly bring on a cough or wheeze in an asthmatic child. There is no need to demonstrate variable peak flow in order to make the diagnosis, as one might in adults. Children with mild asthma may have a quite audible wheeze and a peak flow that is within the normal range. If there is a personal history of atopy or a family history of asthma or atopy, the index of suspicion must rise.

The need to ask the direct question about previous wheezing cannot be overemphasized as it is frequently not volunteered, even if severe. There can be great differences between parents' attitudes to their child's problems: now and again children are seen for the first time with a chest deformed by chronic asthma although they are attending for an entirely different reason. The explanation offered is often that 'it runs in the family' or 'it isn't causing any trouble' or 'he is expected to grow out of it'. Wheezing may not be apparent at the time and it is by no means easy, even for an experienced practitioner, to spot what is happening.

Diagnostic therapy

Special diagnostic tests are not often required to make a diagnosis, since time and the opportunity to see patients promptly are very powerful investigative tools.

Proving the diagnosis by therapeutic trial is often useful, especially when overt wheezing is absent, for example, in children with persistent nocturnal coughing or mild chronic asthma. Prescribing 20 mg of prednisolone daily for seven days usually produces such striking clinical improvement in asthmatic children that it causes all concerned to realize how much better things can be and serves as a spur to ensure that adequate control is achieved by some means other than oral steroids.

Similarly, reversal of wheezing by the administration of an inhaled bronchodilator in the clinic or by the demonstration of an improved peak flow rate will also make the diagnosis plain, but this should be unnecessary in most cases since wheezing usually means asthma. However, it may serve to demonstrate to the parents the ease and effectiveness of bronchodilator therapy. Care must be taken to ensure success as failure to respond may be counterproductive.

The only other condition that causes wheeziness that a family doctor will see frequently is bronchiolitis. It may be prolonged but not recurrent (see page 94). Other causes of wheezing are rare but should not be ignored. None of them respond significantly to bronchodilators, the most useful practical distinction.

GETTING THE BEST FROM DRUGS

There is much misunderstanding over the use of inhaled bronchodilators and oral steroids. These topics are covered on pages 43 to 68, but some generalizations about their application in general practice may be useful.

Bronchodilator drugs

All patients who are asthmatic, however mildly, should have rapid access to a bronchodilator. This usually means having a bronchodilator aerosol in the home, although an oral preparation may be adequate for the very young. It is all too easy for mildly asthmatic patients to have lost or run out of bronchodilator drugs, and doctors frequently see patients whose attack could have been aborted if a bronchodilator had been available. If attacks are frequent, the child should have several inhalers: one at home, one at school and one spare.

Bronchodilators are best administered topically. With few exceptions, asthmatics of four years of age and upwards can use some sort of inhalation device (see Figure 5.3 on page 47) and this should be the normal means of administration. The only disadvantage is that it requires much more effort on the part of the doctor or nurse to explain, demonstrate and check its use. Whoever takes on this essential task should be well versed in the techniques for all the available devices. Surveys have shown that most doctors are themselves unable to use inhaler devices in the approved way.[7] The correct techniques are by no means always logical or obvious, and it is unfair to deny asthmatics the necessary tuition.

Most childhood asthma is precipitated by relatively mild viral respiratory infections. It has been my practice to recommend that when children prone to wheezing develop such infections they should start to use their bronchodilator on a regular basis—that is, every 4 hours from the very start of the infection. I believe this works as an effective prophylactic. A great deal of incapacitating asthma results from starting therapy too late.

Dosage   Trying to cope with acute asthma on four doses of bronchodilator a day can be impossible. As the asthma gets worse, airflow decreases and less drug reaches the lungs. These drugs are remarkably safe in doses higher than those recommended, so, although two puffs of an aerosol or one powder capsule may be sufficient when the inspiratory airflow is high, a double dose may be required (repeated every 2–3 hours) as the asthma gets worse. These higher than usual doses of inhaled bronchodilator are acceptable provided they produce relief. If three or four inhaled doses are given over 2 or 3 min, it is surprising how often a wheeze of several days' standing will virtually disappear within a minute or so. Patients who suddenly find themselves wheezing severely can follow a similar procedure themselves by taking a dose every 10 min for half an hour and then subsequently every 3–4 hours. If this is not adequate, the doctor should be notified without delay. A good rule of thumb is to allow the patient ten capsules of powder or twenty puffs of an aerosol in 24 hours.

Nebulizers in general practice

A nebulizer is an essential piece of equipment for the comprehensive management of asthma.[8] It provides the only means of delivering a topical bronchodilator to children under four years of age who lack the coordination to use any other inhalation device, and almost every doctor will have some such patients. The nebulizer may need to be used frequently throughout an attack; without one the asthma will either be inadequately treated or the patient will have to go to hospital for nebulizer therapy.[9] Oral bronchodilators will, however, be sufficient for most episodes of wheezing in this age group.

Nebulizers are also the most effective way of treating a severe attack of asthma when the child is unfamiliar with inhalers. The high dosage delivered may be effective in dealing with other acute episodes of severe asthma characterized by very low airflow rates since nebulizers will often penetrate the lungs sufficiently where powder and aerosols fail.

This latter situation is unfortunately seen fairly frequently in general practice, and it usually implies poor management by the patient or the doctor. The proper sequence of events should be for the patient to seek medical advice as soon as his bronchodilator inhaler fails to give adequate or sustained relief, at which point oral steroids are usually required.

When patients are lent nebulizers for independent use at home, they must be given adequate instructions on what to expect from nebulizer treatment, and when and how to contact the doctor if expected relief is not obtained.[10,11] Nebulizers do not change the principles of asthma management; they simply act as an alternative means of giving a high dose of a bronchodilator—these drugs do not always work.

It should be noted that spacer devices, particularly large ones incorporating one-way valves, work as well as nebulizers in most cases if similar doses (five to ten puffs) are given.[12] Coordination is a problem for many children but it may be an effective alternative to a nebulizer for older children. The aerosol end of a Volumatic or an improvised spacer made from a plastic cup,[13] bag,[14] or medical record envelope placed close to a younger child's nose or mouth works just as well in most cases. These techniques are useful in general practice because many children require only one such dose burst, after which they can often cope on oral treatment or a standard inhaler. In these cases, the implication is again that treatment has been started too late.

Steroid therapy

A short, sharp course of prednisolone, such as 30 mg in a single morning dose for seven days, will almost invariably terminate an attack of asthma which is unresponsive to bronchodilators in children over two years of age. This dosage for this length of time does not need to be tailed off. Such therapy has a negligible risk of side-effects, unless repeated more than eight times a year.

Peak flow meters

Parents of children prone to severe asthma or those on prophylactic drugs should be encouraged to obtain a peak flow meter (available at a reduced cost through some drug companies or the Asthma Society). These parents need to be taught to identify slowly deteriorating asthma at an early stage and how to use the meter to measure the severity and hence the urgency for medical treatment. Children who are too young to use a peak flow meter should be taught as soon as they are able.

Children with intermittent asthma need to have their peak flow measured in between attacks, the shape of the chest observed for stigmata of chronic airways obstruction, and the chest auscultated. Specific questions should also be asked to exclude the possibility of chronicity.

MANAGEMENT OF SEVERE ASTHMA

Acute severe asthma which is uncontrollable needs urgent referral to hospital. Subsequent management has been dealt with in Chapter 10, but there are important principles that family doctors should adhere to:

- Very little harm can be done by overtreatment, but much harm can be done by undertreatment; therefore, if in doubt, overtreat.

- It is better to admit a child to hospital for management if
  a)   There is any doubt about the severity of attack
  b)   There is a danger that the situation might deteriorate seriously
  c)   Parents cannot be relied upon to recognize the important signs of deterioration.

Hospital admission for reasons of social inadequacy or the avoidance of life-threatening situations that may arise are perfectly valid.

MANAGEMENT OF CHRONIC DISEASE

The management of childhood asthma involves a partnership of three: the doctor who is the expert medical resource, the child who has the disease, and the parents who are responsible for the child's medication compliance and general care. The dynamics of this partnership can never be static. The balance will shift between members according to the expertise and competence of each, and the age of the child. With time, the responsibility should pass from the doctor to the parents and subsequently to the child. The rate of flow of information will depend on the patient's experience with asthma and the willingness of the doctor to share information about management.

The doctor and parents

Most parents thirst for information, especially when their child is first diagnosed. This opportunity should be grasped to enable the parents to take more responsibility for the child's own management; it will relieve all parties of much anxiety. Use may also be made of other sources of expert knowledge. There are many publications about asthma produced both by drug companies and, in the UK, by the regional offices of the Asthma Society. But before handing out this information to parents, the doctor should familiarize himself with the contents and ensure that he agrees with them since contradictions only damage confidence.

Some parents become very well informed about illness and its management and may have a healthy scepticism about the right of doctors to dictate treatment. It is all too easy to respond to such attitudes with unnecessary defensiveness. More often than not, the goals of the parents and doctors are identical, but misunderstandings arise because these goals and the means of attaining them are not discussed. Some doctors resent the fact that parents seem to be as knowledgeable as themselves about certain aspects of their child's disease. They should not be worried by this; such parents will not usually expect the doctor to know everything but will value his overall knowledge perspective and experience.

At the other end of the spectrum are parents who have no inclination to take responsibility for their child's asthma. This may be because of an innate complacency, or because they have never had experience of taking responsibility for such things. But given encouragement and interest from the doctor, these parents can be stimulated to take a more active role.

Parents have their own ideas about disease, its aetiology and treatment—'health beliefs'. Many hold health beliefs which are incorrect and the flow of information between parents and doctor will make little headway unless care is taken to discover and correct them.[15] For example, advice from a doctor to use a bronchodilator inhaler at the start of a respiratory infection is unlikely to be complied with if the parents believe that the drugs should be saved for times when wheezing is very severe because the body becomes resistant to the drugs. There are many such false health beliefs about asthma and they are not simply confined to patients or parents!

Specific knowledge required by parents

Parents need to know the names, functions and effects of the drugs that their child is using. Below are some examples of information that parents may need to know:

- The effect of a bronchodilator should be almost immediate and should last for about 4 hours
- A preventer drug has a very slow onset of action and needs to be taken regularly and continually, regardless of whether the symptoms are present
- When an emergency supply of steroids is given, there will be a delay of several hours before the drugs take effect. Anticipating a severe attack of asthma is therefore necessary for their most effective use
- How to recognize serious asthma and what to do about it: signs to be aware of include waking at night because of wheezing, a morning wheeze persisting for hours, inability to perform normal activities because of wheezing, failure to respond to the bronchodilator, and a slow deterioration over several days.

If these situations arise, parents should seek help quickly; in practice, this usually means on the same day or even immediately. This degree of access should be assured, and reception staff should be prepared to recognize that asthmatic patients need to be seen with urgency on request.

Most patients who present to the doctor with acute severe asthma have had the warning signs for some days, and many of these serious situations could be averted if patients responded within hours of recognizing the signs of deterioration. The doctor could then act promptly within a similar time, initiating appropriate therapy, such as steroids, without having to dash out to the emergency of acute severe asthma. The key is educating the patient and parents to recognize the signs, and it is not sufficient simply to give them this information without checking whether they have understood it. Doctors often expect too much in this respect. It is usually necessary to write down important points for patients and parents to take away and refer to when necessary. The most effective and efficient way of teaching patients about asthma self-care is unknown. Structured programmes for individuals have made little headway and are very time-consuming.[16,17] It is probable that such methods are too doctor-centred and that more attention to the patient's wider personal needs is necessary.[18]

The doctor and patient

When all is said and done, the disease belongs to the patient and not the doctor. A patient who is able to make rational decisions, therefore, has the right to determine the goals, and in most cases, the patient's are identical to the doctor's: minimize symptoms, avoid life-threatening situations, minimize interference with normal life, and avoid medication hazards.

Many consultations for asthma will reveal misconceptions that, when corrected, will improve the patient's capability of managing better next time. All doctors share this teaching responsibility, whether they are general, community or hospital practitioners. If the doctor were to ask himself at the end of each episode, 'What has the patient learned from this experience?' would it be something positive?

The relationship between doctor and patient in the management of chronic disease is a difficult balancing act. On the one hand, the doctor does not want the patient to become dependent, as this prevents him from becoming responsible for his own problems and imposes unreasonable work on the doctor. On the other hand, human beings have a surprising capacity to come to terms with affliction. So the ones that are too dependent need discouraging from over-reliance, and those that are too independent need firm supervision. Perhaps the most difficult patient is the complacent one who seems unconcerned about the treatment or the disease. When adults fall into this category, it is easier because they have the right to reject advice, but, with a child, it is more serious. If neither parent can be persuaded of the need to treat and supervize the child's asthma, then caring professionals, such as health visitors, school nurses and teachers, may be able to assist by being on the look out for neglected disease.

A more pernicious situation sometimes occurs when a child's asthma is used as a scapegoat for family tensions, or may even be the cause of them if asthma is regarded as a sign of weakness. In other cases, treatment may be withheld in order to 'score' off some member of the family. Fortunately most of these situations arise in children with mild asthma. In other cases, it may be worth while considering the involvement of hospital services. This could elevate the problem to a higher degree of seriousness in the parents' eyes and make them behave more responsibly.

Problems of adolescence

A great many asthmatic children improve as they get older and leave their asthma behind them, although for some this is only temporary. But adolescence can give rise to a new set of problems, particularly for the parents who lose control of treatment—this is sometimes used as an instrument in the acquisition of independence. It may be necessary for the parents and the doctor to accept temporary loss of control of the asthma during this period. It is often best to remove all responsibility for treatment from the parents and place it on the patient. Parents should be advised not to interfere, except in an emergency, and the patient must be told that his parents have agreed to this. The dangers of asthma and the need for constant supervision and treatment if it is getting out of control should be explained and the patient allowed more responsibility than is perhaps deserved. Freedom to control symptoms is then preserved, with full realization that failure to treat can end in tragedy. An emergency course of steroids for circumstances when help may not be immediately available, and advice to go straight to hospital with serious problems, may also be useful.

The doctor and the hospital service

Parents are sometimes seduced by the assuredness and technology aspects of hospitals and go to an accident and emergency department rather than to their own doctor. The parents and the hospital staff may be tempted to make a scapegoat of the family doctor who is apparently unable or unwilling to provide the necessary treatment. The uncomfortable truth may be that the parents have left it too late to seek help and know that a reprimand from their doctor may result (given not out of malice but to improve future management). Proper use of medical services needs to be taught. The family doctor ought to be the key worker in the community management of asthma; the hospital can provide expertise in cases of difficult diagnosis or management, and high technology care for serious disease. These two sides of care ought to be complementary, but in reality often act independently.[19] More personal contact between primary and secondary carers could reduce this problem.

The need for hospital referral

Family doctors cannot be expected to be as expert at treating asthma as specialists, and sometimes the gap is very wide. But referral of patients to specialists in the course of a chronic disease needs special consideration. Most chronic diseases are managed in general practice, and asthma in children is no exception. For most, hospitals offer no advantage over treatment by the family doctor in cases of mild to moderate disease which responds well to appropriate therapy. Neither should it be necessary to refer patients for diagnosis, as this can almost always be made from the history alone. Asthma may be more difficult to diagnose in children with another pre-existing disease, as it may be uncertain whether it is part of the underlying disease or a new disease process.

When the diagnosis of a chronic or recurring disease is made, parents may feel unhappy and want to seek a second opinion; or they may feel that asthma is something which ought to be managed by a hospital. The practitioner must make up his own mind about seeking a second opinion but the purpose must be clearly stated in the referral letter, so that the child can be quickly discharged from the clinic.

Very young children may benefit from referral as they are difficult to diagnose and there is limited treatment available. Likewise, children with very severe or very brittle asthma who are known to become critical quickly may need rapid admission to hospital.[20] Many hospitals allow such patients direct access to a hospital ward on request. Obviously they will be under hospital supervision. Children with severe asthma may also need to be referred for assessment of growth and drug therapy, particularly if oral steroids are required.

Discharge and interim letters should provide information about *why* certain things are done rather than simply *what* is done. The discharge letter is a good way of conveying educational information—it is a document whose potential in this respect is usually neglected but is surely enormous. Even positive critical comment when management had been inappropriate might be acceptable, but only from a consultant. Patients often see hospital doctors as too busy to be asked questions and rely on the family doctor to fill in the details. This is impossible unless the information is there. The rationale behind a particular course of treatment may be obvious to the doctor writing the letter, but not to the general practitioner who may be unfamiliar with this particular clinic's ways.

Patients sometimes seem to get trapped by outpatient departments, and are given unnecessary follow-up appointments because the doctor seeing the patient (perhaps never the same one twice) is unsure why he is being followed up at all, and has insufficient confidence to discharge him. Family doctors may be reluctant to take over medical management while a patient feels that he is 'under the hospital'. To prevent this, patients should be discharged at the earliest opportunity. This would help to avoid the situation where everybody thinks somebody else is in charge!

ALTERNATIVE THERAPIES

Parents of children with troublesome asthma are likely, at some stage, to consider unorthodox treatment from doctors or alternative practitioners. Doctors have a responsibility to point out the possible advantages and disadvantages, and to warn against exploitation and the other dangers that the patient may experience. These dangers will generally be ones of omission, for example, innocently leaving off an important treatment in order to try something new. Even though the doctor may feel irritated by this rejection of treatment, the best interests of the patient will be served by maintaining a friendly relationship. If the alternative treatment fails to produce improvement, orthodox therapy can continue.

The word 'allergy' (see page 4) used in connection with asthma often triggers parents to seek alternative treatments. Specific desensitizations are generally disappointing unless the asthma is caused by a single treatable allergen. Such patients are rare since most are atopic and allergic to a wide variety of common allergens. It is worth pointing out to parents that even if desensitization can be contemplated, conventional therapy with drugs is simpler and more comfortable, and remains under *their* control.

Exclusion diets

Some parents may want to try exclusion diets and there is no reason why the family doctor should not guide the parents through an experimental diet excluding common food allergens such as dairy produce, eggs and yeast, or free of additives and salicylates. In knowledgeable hands, such diets can sometimes produce improvements but, when applied by parents without supervision, they are often ineffective, or may even lead to dietary inadequacy. It is usual practice to maintain the child on the diet for a period of three weeks, time enough to observe any improvement in symptoms. If improvement occurs, new foods can be introduced one at a time about every three days and recurrence of symptoms documented. Proof of the connection depends on being able to reproduce the results by challenge with the suspected offending food. Most children fail to improve on such regimes but many doctors will know of children who have appeared to benefit. It is not, however, part of usual asthma management to give these measures priority and the variability of asthma makes dietary measures very difficult to interpret.

REVIEW PROCEDURES

Every patient with asthma needs to be reviewed regularly, but the means of achieving this will vary from one practice to another. Few practitioners will have the space, staff or inclination to set up a special clinic and, in a sense, this excludes one of the great advantages of general practice, namely that the patient and the doctor are known to each other—a relationship that ensures management is tailored to the needs of the individual patient. Some general practitioners find a special asthma clinic, often run by a nurse, more effective,[21] and many others are copying this model. Many asthma patients can be reviewed opportunistically when they come to the surgery for treatment of their asthma or some other problem, but this system can be unreliable when the pressures of practice do not allow adequate priority to be given to the matter. It can be made efficient by using a check list in the patient's records, but this needs to be combined with some alerting mechanism for periods when there are no consultations. For example, a repeat prescription system could be made to alert the doctor after a specific time interval, and the records could then be checked to see if the review had been undertaken. This still does not detect those patients who have asthma but have received no treatment. A disease index would take care of this problem. This might consist of cards recording the name, address and date of birth of each patient and a code or disease name, so that the cards could be filed in disease order. The medical record could then be conspicuously marked with the same code and the date of entry on the index. Such an index takes time to build up but by combining information from repeat prescriptions, memory and opportunistic identification, an effective register can be started. Quality of care evaluations can then be made by systematic examination of the records, identified via the index to find out whether monitoring objectives are being achieved.

Review objectives

These vary from patient to patient according to the severity of the asthma, intelligence, social circumstances and so on. Inhaler technique and drug treatment need to be checked, as does morbidity. Absenteeism from school is an important measure of this, as are the attitudes of the parents and child to the disease. Most children with asthma do not need any more time off school than non-asthmatics. If this is not the case, then either the management or the parents' attitude needs looking at. Most episodes of wheezing are brought on by respiratory infections which, if adequately treated with bronchodilators from the beginning, will last no longer for an asthmatic child than for any other child. Questions should be asked about sport and exercise as these may be a more sensitive measure than time off school.

Morbidity may need to be quantified accurately and history may be inadequate because of differing expectations. Symptom diaries can overcome this. A daily record is kept of the amount of coughing and wheezing, and of activities that may be limited by asthma. Drug use is also recorded and the skill in their use can be determined. It is also useful for measuring progress and judging severity.

Children with chronic asthma need to have their rate of growth recorded because it may be adversely affected. This particularly applies to those few children needing continuous oral steroids, who will usually be under the care of a hospital.

It would be inappropriate to lay down specified intervals at which children should be reviewed; this will depend on the methods used for reviewing and the fail-safe systems which are in operation. The opportunities which exist for detecting problems in general practice are vast and there is no single foolproof system. The most important factor is the doctor, who should maintain a questioning and critical attitude.

Schools, health visitors and nurses will be involved in the care of asthmatic children. What is their attitude to asthma? Does it coincide with the doctor's own? Do the schools allow free access to bronchodilators during school hours or are they confiscated and returned at the end of the day? The help of these people will be invaluable when reviewing the children of irresponsible parents, so the benefits of cooperation are mutual. We should not forget the inverse care law which states that the ones most in need of care are the ones least likely to be receiving it. With children, this places more responsibility on the doctor to seek them out.

Asthma in children is, by and large, a simple disease to treat. It is so common that it can only be adequately treated if family doctors do it.[22] The key to starting is identification and naming of the disease. The key to continuing is monitoring and evaluation of care.

PRACTICAL POINTS

- Most asthmatic children can be cared for by their family doctor.

- Early diagnosis of asthma is very important.

- All asthmatic patients should have rapid access to a bronchodilator.

- A nebulizer is an essential piece of equipment.

- If in doubt, admit the patient to hospital.

- The doctor should involve patients and parents as much as possible in the management of asthma.

- Family doctors should cooperate closely with hospitals, social services and schools.

- An adequate review procedure for asthmatic patients should be implemented.

12
Clinical case histories

Although the underlying problem, that of abnormal airways lability, is common to all asthmatic children, there is considerable variation in the pattern of presentation. For this reason, five case histories and one parent's story have been included to illustrate the range of clinical presentation.

SHARON

Sharon first had an attack of coughing and wheezing at the age of six months. This was put down to teething, and settled after four days. Over the next nine months she had four similar episodes, each coming on within one to two days of the onset of nasal discharge and mild pyrexia. A diagnosis of wheezy bronchitis was made by their family doctor and antibiotics were prescribed for each of these episodes. At the age of eighteen months, her parents first noticed that she tended to cough and wheeze on running around when she had an upper respiratory tract infection, but at other times was entirely asymptomatic.

The pattern of illness remained largely unchanged over the next four years but her parents requested referral to a specialist as Sharon had to stay at home for several days whenever she had a cold and her parents considered that 'the antibiotics were no longer working'. Sharon's mother was also chesty as a child, but had grown out of her symptoms by the age of eleven years. On examination Sharon was of normal height and weight and had minimal deformity with mild bilateral Harrison sulci. Clinically there was no evidence of airways obstruction but her peak flow rose from 160 l/min to 210 l/min after inhaling 400 µg of salbutamol from a Rotahaler. Skin tests showed a mild positive reaction to house dust, house dust mite, cats and pollens.

Case commentary

There is no doubt from the history and the response to beta$_2$ stimulants that Sharon has asthma. Although she does have allergic tendencies (positive skin tests), the sole trigger for her problem seems to be that of viral upper respiratory tract infections and exercise. This is the commonest of all presentations. Response to therapy is likely to be excellent, and it may be sufficient for her to take inhaled bronchodilator therapy when symptoms are present. If not, her response to prophylactic therapy (sodium cromoglycate or topical steroids) is likely to be dramatic.

KATY

Katy was born at term and was entirely well until the age of twelve weeks when she became acutely ill over a period of three days with a runny nose, tachypnoea and difficulty in feeding. On admission to hospital, she was found to be mildly cyanosed and hyperinflated, and had fine crepitations throughout her lung fields with high-pitched inspiratory and expiratory rhonchi. Respiratory syncytial virus was found within cells in nasal secretions using an immunofluorescence technique. A diagnosis of acute bronchiolitis was made. She required tube feeding and oxygen for five days and then appeared to recover completely.

Over the next two years, she had episodes of coughing and wheezing whenever she caught a cold. The cough was particularly troublesome at night, and at the age of eighteen months she had to be admitted to hospital as she was acutely breathless. She then responded dramatically to nebulized salbutamol. Between attacks she seemed to be entirely well with a normal chest x-ray. Her blood eosinophil count was not elevated, and all skin tests were negative.

Case commentary

Seventy-five per cent of children who are admitted to hospital with RSV bronchiolitis will have further episodes of wheezing and coughing.[1] These symptoms can be severe but are not particularly associated with an atopic tendency in the child or a family history of either atopy or abnormal airways lability.[2] Most will apparently grow out of their symptoms by the age of five years. Response to antiasthma therapy is almost always excellent once the child is over the age of fifteen months. It is likely that the acute episode of RSV bronchiolitis is responsible for abnormal airways lability persisting for several years. It is possible, however, that these children had abnormally sensitive airways before their contact with RSV and therefore finished up in hospital.

DAVID

David first wheezed at the age of eighteen months. Since then he has been rarely free of symptoms. He wakes most nights with coughing and wheezing. Although he takes part in all games at school and manages to cope, he is always in goal when on the football field and enjoys swimming rather than other physical acitivities. He misses approximately five weeks of school attendance every term and is beginning to fall behind in his education as a result. He has been admitted to hospital with severe asthma on six occasions, and on four of these required intravenous steroids. He avoids cats, as contact leads to the development of a severe urticarial rash on his face and eyelids within a few minutes, followed by conjunctivitis, rhinitis and an acute asthma attack. Despite this obvious allergic tendency, all his previous hospital admissions have been provoked by viral upper respiratory tract infections. His height is on the third centile and he has considerable chest deformity with bilateral Harrison sulci and protuberance of the upper sternum (see Figure 12.1). Despite this, he considers his asthma is reasonably well controlled, and complains little.

Case commentary

David has severe asthma and tolerates a considerable degree of airways obstruction. He is probably hypoxic at least some of the night and needs additional therapy to improve his enjoyment of life. His response to sodium cromoglycate is likely to be inadequate and he will almost certainly require regular inhaled topical steroids and beta$_2$ stimulants for many years.

RICHARD

Richard thrived up to the age of ten months. His parents then found that he tended to become acutely breathless after crawling around on the floor. This was not associated with any coughing or wheezing. By the age of eighteen months the breathlessness, brought on now by running around, was often accompanied by cyanosis. He was admitted to the local hospital where he was observed to have an attack. The paediatrician's impression was that he had a severe upper airways obstruction, but laryngoscope and bronchoscopy two days later revealed no abnormality. When seen in the referral unit, he was noted to be well-grown and healthy and to have no obvious chest deformity. As formal exercise tests were impractical, the staff played football with him in the hospital corridor. Ten minutes later his mother announced that an attack was coming on. The clinical findings were those of breathlessness, mild cyanosis, rapidly progressing hyperinflation and only quiet high-pitched rhonchi on inspiration and expiration. The attack was terminated within 3 min by giving salbutamol respirator solution via a nebulizer.

Case commentary

Richard has severe EIB as the only manifestation of his asthma. The site of origin of the obstruction is mostly in the small airways, leading to severe hyperinflation rather than coughing and wheezing. Response to prophylactic therapy (nebulized sodium cromoglycate) was gratifyingly excellent. Although EIB is usually only one of a number of triggers, there are children who have this as their sole asthmatic manifestation.[3] A small number of children have symptoms that are brought on purely by exposure to very cold air.[4]

JANE

Jane was first admitted to hospital at the age of two-and-a-half years. At this time she was critically ill. She had a weak rapid pulse, looked very pale and had rapid grunting respiration. Her left lung was dull to percussion and, on

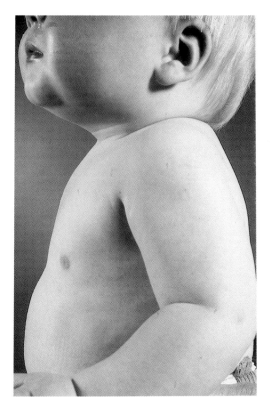

Figure 12.1 The upper part of this child's chest
protrudes due to lung hyperinflation.

auscultation, crepitations could be heard all over the lung fields but more on
the left than the right. Bronchial breathing was also noted over the left chest.
The cardiac apex and trachea were not obviously deviated. A chest x-ray
confirmed that she had massive consolidation of her left lung (see Figure 12.2).
A diagnosis of acute bacterial pneumonia was made and she was given oxygen
therapy, intravenous flucloxacillin, ampicillin and hydrocortisone. The
following day she had improved dramatically. Her left lung was clear but her
right upper lobe showed signs of collapse and consolidation on x-ray. Her only
significant past history was that she tended to cough and wheeze whenever
she had a cold.

Case commentary

Jane illustrates a small group of children who for some reason produce large quantities
of secretion as part of their asthma syndrome. These children tend to have recurrent
episodes of collapse/consolidation up to the age of three to four years and then revert to
a more normal asthmatic pattern with coughing and wheezing in response to infections,
colds and sometimes allergic triggers. Once identified, these very worrying attacks can
usually be relieved by treatment with nebulized beta$_2$ stimulants, accompanied if
necessary by systemic steroids.

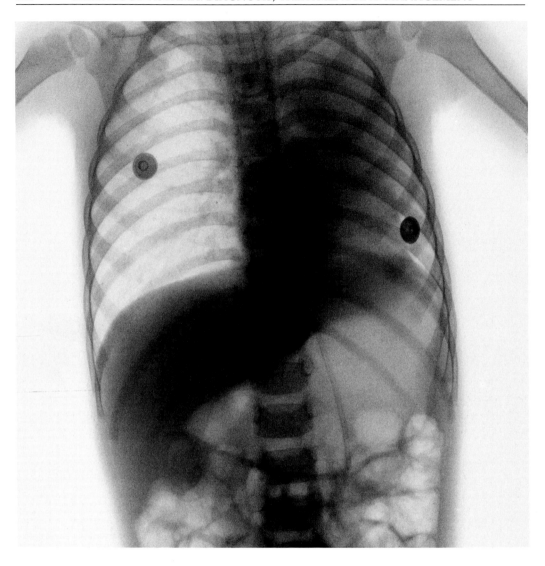

Figure 12.2 A massive collapse of the left lung in an asthmatic child aged two years.

A PARENT'S STORY

As doctors, we are often worried about children's asthma symptoms, but it is only by asking parents about how they envisage their child's condition that we can get a true picture of the impact of asthma on family life. For this reason we have included Gregory's story, as reported by his mother. This is a fairly extreme story and by no means typical, but it does serve to illustrate a number of points at the same time.

Gregory was a normal baby apart from being able to catch cold at the drop of a hat. At seventeen months, the wheeze crept in, and the habit of waking up at 5 o'clock in the morning. When he was two years old, his sister, Vicky, was born, an event which heralded the beginning of a year that I would like to forget. Gregory was frequently ill, waking in the night, coughing. My husband and I took it in turns to walk round the room with him but no matter how little he had slept in the night, come 5 o'clock, his day started. Vicky would wake up for feeds and have difficulty in going back to sleep—later it was teething troubles. It got to the point when a whole night's sleep was non-existent for us. Obviously this did have a large bearing on our reaction to Gregory's illness.

Just before Gregory's third birthday, our local doctor, Dr Brown, decided it was necessary to send Gregory to hospital because he was particularly ill at the time. We were shocked, both having had healthy childhoods—we thought that hospital seemed a rather desperate measure to take. We did realize Gregory was very ill and the hospital doctors confirmed this but we were horrified by the oxygen tent which gave us little, if any, physical contact with Gregory who we felt needed our physical reassurance. It was even more shattering when we had to leave him there for the night. If we hadn't been so physically tired, we would have had no sleep worrying. After a harrowing four days, Gregory came home but he was listless and would not eat—that just meant changing one worry for another. I must emphasize at this point that our doctor was very helpful and never queried being called out; he even came when I told him about Gregory's listlessness and made friends with Gregory. (Gregory hadn't been feeling particularly friendly towards the doctor knowing he was responsible for his stay in hospital.)

When we returned to the hospital outpatients department for a checkup, we were told the diagnosis of Gregory's problem was asthma. To us, asthma meant wheezing old men, and our ignorance on the subject was absolute. But we did realize that it was likely to prove a longterm thing, possibly for life, and this raised a whole host of new spectres.

The first ten to twelve months after Gregory had been diagnosed as asthmatic were the worst, I think. Not only was Gregory in hospital seven times but we seemed to be in the middle of a tug of war. On the one hand, Dr Brown would be against sending Gregory to hospital, something we agreed with on the whole. But on the other hand, the doctors in the hospital would always ask why we had left it so long before bringing Gregory in. The tug of war would start with Gregory catching a cold and having a sleepless night. We would call the doctor in the morning and he would visit about noon and give us a prescription for some medicines. At 7 pm, we would have to call the doctor again because Gregory's condition would have deteriorated—the doctor would then advise us to send him to hospital. He wouldn't agree to send him in earlier; the hospital doctors would complain; we would feel guilty and so on. At one stage, Dr Brown suggested we only wanted to send Gregory to hospital so that we could get a good night's sleep, and in a way it was true.

In July, the hospital decided Gregory's problem warranted a case conference. A social worker was sent round to check up on us—we liked to think it wasn't to check whether we were being good parents to Gregory but it certainly felt like that. It also raised questions in our own minds—were we neglecting Gregory or Vicky? Were we being ideal parents?

I had always felt that Gregory's sleeplessness had something to do with a course of vitamins he was taking at the time, but in August there was a big improvement in his sleeping and eating patterns and he started to put on weight. Not for long, however, because in September Gregory was in the intensive care unit, and to add to the worry, I had to look after Vicky at the same time. Previously when Gregory was in hospital I had taken Vicky with me on daily visits because I didn't like imposing on neighbours continually. She was happier with this arrangement too because she didn't like being parted from me. But this time the playroom nurses rang to ask if I could collect Vicky who was rather upset, so I had to leave Gregory earlier than planned, which then upset him.

In November the case conference was held. We never really found out what it hoped to achieve because we were excluded from attending—was that really necessary? The only thing that was achieved, as far as we know, was that we could bypass our own doctor and call an ambulance on our own authority. While seeming to solve one problem, this gave us the added burden of not abusing this gift.

November proved to be the turning point for a number of other problems. Gregory was physically improving and we were fast catching up on our lost sleep, which helped considerably. My husband was promoted and given a rise which helped to improve our financial position. A child in hospital is a continual drain on financial as well as physical resources and that year we got very low on both. The social worker who visited in July did give us some hope of financial assistance, but though Gregory was placed on the physically handicapped list (and is still there as far as we know), the only assistance was the loan of a rubber mattress for his bed. This, although useful, did not help the budget greatly.

On many occasions, the worse thing was not knowing what to do when, at 2 o'clock in the morning (it was always in the early hours) Gregory was poorly, his breathing painful to listen to and his bodily struggles to keep breathing equally painful to watch. Then the decision to send him to hospital or not, but the loneliness of that time of night was quite something. You would look out of the window and it seemed that the rest of the world slept, oblivious to your predicament.

I have mentioned the main problems, but there were other minor ones, for example, the attitude of other people. The mention of asthma immediately provoked a rush of stories of asthmatic children other people had known who had grown out of it. Children, according to different informants, grew out of asthma at the age of five, six, seven—in fact, any age up to twenty years. We told Gregory that it was unlikely that he would grow out of his asthma, but if he did, it was a bonus: in other words he should expect to have it for life. A helpful relative would claim that we weren't looking after Gregory correctly just because we let him play in the garden on a lovely hot day a couple of days after he had come out of hospital! Other people told us of asthmatics cured by a herbalist, a holiday in Switzerland or drinking goat's milk instead of cow's milk. This was more insidious as we wondered if these cures would work for Gregory and felt guilty when we did not try them.

Guilt is a word I haven't mentioned, but it played a big part in my thoughts. However irrational it is, there's still a feeling of guilt that Gregory probably 'inherited' his asthma from me. Then again, did I set too high a standard for him when he was a baby? Have I shown favouritism to one child at the expense of the other?

After that first year, we were better able to cope. Gregory was much fitter in appearance, he was able to cope more himself and was aware of his limitations. The problems were not so much on the surface any more. The main problem was trying to give Gregory a normal life and not being over-protective: not being too anxious to look for signs and symptoms, and yet avoiding a repetition of his 'collapse' last year; we had to learn that there were no hard and fast rules with asthma, that no two attacks were identical. It was a great help that we could call on one of the doctors in the children's department if we were in difficulties, and I really cannot express how much of a morale boost this knowledge gave us. The future presented some big question marks—how was it going to affect his working life? If he married, what were the chances of his children getting it? More immediately, what about school trips abroad or even days out camping with the Scouts? Was he always to be tied to a nebulizer? The nebulizer had helped considerably, but it was a tie, and life tended to revolve around it. It was even difficult going out to tea: the nebulizer had to come along too and it weighed a ton. Still, the way technology was progressing, I was sure that something else would come up soon enough. We were greatly disturbed at the high level of drugs he had to take, and wondered if it was a sign that his asthma was getting worse. How much worse could it get? The special school down in the south of England loomed darkly at this time.

Five or six years elapsed and life improved greatly for us all. Regular admissions to the hospital became a thing of the past, and in the six years Gregory was on the nebulizer, he went into hospital twice—a marked improvement on the three or four times a year prior to that.

We found that schools were helpful to a degree. By this I mean that the primary teachers would help with medications, excusing games and so on, but were helpless when it came to Gregory having an attack of asthma at school. The secondary school was a great improvement, as there was a trained nurse on the premises and the school was not frightened by the responsibility.

Gregory's first year at secondary school was distinctly fraught. Every time he fell over he was in great pain, as though he had broken a bone. That year, we collected four slings and a variety of leg bandages. Eventually we discovered he had a hairline fracture in each heel and was unable to walk. By the beginning of December, he had both legs in plaster and one wrist strapped up. Then he had a very bad night with his asthma, and the next day his other wrist was hurting him. At this stage I rang up the hospital demanding that he was admitted as I just couldn't cope. Once in the ward his asthma grew worse and by evening he was on a drip. But the increase of steroids helped his bone trouble and just before Christmas he was out of hospital and his plasters. In the middle of January we saw it all start again, first one heel then the other. This time he was given splints which could be taken off at night—a great improvement.

Again, we experienced problems with differences of opinion over the cause of Gregory's bone trouble. The bone specialist said it was due to the low dosage of steroids taken every other day for his asthma. The asthma specialist felt that such a low dosage could do not harm, even though Gregory had been on the course for five years or so. Eventually we took the decision to take Gregory off the steroids, keeping them in reserve for an attack. After that Gregory had no further trouble with his legs, even though he fell over innumerable times, like most children.

During this time, the school was most cooperative again. In the November and December, they arranged a home tutor but by January the school had acquired a nebulizer so a taxi collected Gregory in the morning and returned him in the evening, and the nebulizer was administered at lunchtime or any other time it was needed.

Gregory is now fifteen-and-a-half years old, and for several months has been so fit that he no longer needs the nebulizer; it was a great day when we were able to return it to the hospital. He is nearly 6 feet tall and, if he ever makes the 6 feet 4 inches that the hospital said he would have reached had he not been on steroids, Mother is crying no tears over that—it's not easy trying to clothe that height! Football is his hobby and when he returns home after training on a very cold night, or a six-mile run in the pouring rain, I say a silent 'Thank you, God'. To my mind, the age of miracles is not past.

Case Commentary

Gregory's story indicates that he has had severe asthma. There were a number of ways in which management had been suboptimal. His family did not find out the diagnosis of asthma until he had been discharged from hospital. The role of the case conference was apparently not made clear to the family, that is, it was set up to improve communications between the family doctor, the hospital staff and the family so that appropriate strategies could be drawn up. The school teachers in the primary school were unable to cope with acute attacks probably because there was a lack of communication between the hospital staff and the school.

Appendix

The text below is the transcript of a tape prepared for asthmatic children. Tapes provide a useful way of educating children about their condition and reminding them of important treatment points:

'All right, so you've got asthma, but what does that mean and what can you do about it? Well, the answer to the second question is quite a lot. There's no doubt that with a little knowledge about asthma and how to use your treatments, your asthma can be controlled to such an extent that it's little more than a bore, and the aim of this short tape is to fill you in on some of these points.

All the breathing tubes in your chest are surrounded by rings of muscles. These muscles are important, as they tighten if anything particularly nasty is breathed in. This protects your very delicate lungs from damage. The only way an asthmatic person is different is that this tendency for the muscles to tighten is increased, causing first coughing then wheezing and at times difficulty in breathing in and out.

You're likely to find that your asthma is more of a problem when you have a cold, and you may find that at other times you're entirely well. Many people with asthma cough and wheeze for five or ten minutes after running around, particularly when it's cold and windy outside. Wheezing may also be a problem when you breathe in tree and grass pollens. This is likely to be the cause if you find your asthma flares up in the spring or early summer. If cats or dogs bring on an attack, try to avoid close contact with them as much as possible. You may tend to wake up coughing and wheezing at night otherwise. Although children with asthma are certainly not particularly nervous, that unpleasant chestiness often flares up at Christmas time, just before exams or when you're particularly fed up with life at school or at home.

This list seems fairly long, but it's usually very easy to control your asthma so that you can lead an entirely normal life, including joining in with all games. For this you'll need to know how to use your treatments properly. You'll almost certainly have been given an inhaler which delivers medicine to your lungs either as a powder or a fine, dry aerosol spray and you'll have been told to use this whenever your chest feels tight or you're coughing. This medicine is known as a bronchodilator and it acts by causing the tight muscles to relax within two or three minutes, so that you can breathe more easily. There are several examples including Ventolin, Bricanyl and Berotec. The aerosols are not so easy to use without practice and you'll probably need to be shown how to use the gadgets several times to get the maximum benefit.

The main points to remember are that you should first breathe out, place the opening of the aerosol in your mouth and then press down on the canister to fire the dose as you start breathing in, drawing the bronchodilator down into your lungs. The aerosol and powder preparations should give relief within two or three minutes and they're entirely safe; but if you ever find that they don't work or are only lasting two or three hours, you must get help as this is an indication that the asthma attack is slipping out of control and you might need some extra treatment.

The bronchodilator drugs will also stop you wheezing and coughing during games if you take one or two doses immediately before starting. You may have been given the bronchodilator drug in the form of a tablet or syrup. This is rather less effective as it's slower to act but it does last for a longer period and so it may stop you wheezing at night.

For many asthmatic children, extra forms of treatment are necessary. These don't make you feel better within a few minutes as the bronchodilators do, but they do soothe the tubes so that the attacks are then much less likely to come on. They are again usually breathed in as a powder or aerosol using similar gadgets. They're a bit of a bore as they need to be taken regularly every day, whether or not you're wheezing, but they can be very effective. Examples are Intal, Becotide and Pulmicort.

One final point to remember. When you feel an attack coming on, don't panic or get upset. This'll only make the effects of the attack worse. Try and keep calm. Take the medicine you've had prescribed and the attack will go away. If it doesn't, tell your parents or a teacher straight away and they can do something about it.

Asthma is only an ailment. It's not an illness and it doesn't have to stop you doing almost anything you most want to do, so don't let it. Cheerio!'

References

Chapter 1

1. Scadding JG, 'Definition and clinical categories in asthma', in *Asthma* 2nd edn (Eds TJH Clark, S Godfrey, Chapman and Hall, London 1983): pp. 1–11.

2. Lenney W, Milner AD, 'At what age do bronchodilators work?' *Arch Dis Child* (1978) **53:** pp. 532–5.

3. Speight A, Lee DA, Hey EN, 'Underdiagnosis and undertreatment of asthma in childhood', *Br Med J* (1983) **286:** pp. 1253–6.

4. Cockcroft DW, 'Mechanics of perennial allergic asthma', *Lancet* (1983) **ii:** pp. 253–6.

5. Williams HE, Phelan PD, 'The 'missed' inhaled foreign body in children', *Med J Australia* (1969) **1:** p. 625.

6. Smith J, 'Prevalence and natural history of asthma in school children', *Br Med J* (1961) **1:** pp. 711–13.

7. Empey DW, Laitinen LA, Jacobs L, Gold WM, Nadel JA, 'Mechanisms of bronchial hyper-reactivity in normal subjects after URTI', *Am Rev Respir Dis* (1976) **113:** pp. 131–9.

8. Collier AM, Pimmel RL, Hasselblad V *et al*, 'Spirometry changes in normal children with upper respiratory infection', *Am Rev Respir Dis* (1975) **117:** pp. 47–53.

9. Webb MSC, Henry RL, Milner AD, Stokes GM, Swarbrick AS, 'Continuing respiratory problems three and a half years after acute viral bronchiolitis', *Arch Dis Child* (1985) **60:** pp. 1064–7.

10. Pullan CR, Hey EN, 'Wheezing, asthma and pulmonary dysfunction ten years after infection with respiratory syncytial virus in infancy', *Br Med J* (1982) **284:** pp. 1665–9.

11. McConnochie KM, Mark JD, McBride JT, Hall WJ, Miller RL, 'Normal pulmonary function measurements and airways reactivity in childhood after mild bronchiolitis', *J Pediatrics* (1985) **107:** pp. 54–8.

12. Mok JYQ, Waugh PR, Simpson H, '*Mycoplasma pneumoniae* infection—A follow-up study of fifty children with respiratory illness', *Arch Dis Child* (1979) **54:** pp. 506–11.

13. Sears MR, Rea HH, Fenwick J, Beaglehole R, Gillies AJD, Holst PE, O'Donnell TV, Rothwell RPG, Sutherland DC, 'Deaths from asthma in New Zealand', *Arch Dis Child* (1986) **61:** pp. 6–10.

14. Farr RS, Spector SL, *What is asthma? The asthmatic patient in trouble* (CPC Communications Inc Greenwich   1975): p. 35.

15. Marsh DG, Meyers DA, Bias WB, 'The epidemiology and genetics of atopic allergy', *N Eng J Med* (1981) **305:** pp. 1551–9.

16. Moore WJ, Midwinter RE, Morris AF, Colley JRT, Soothill JF, 'Infant feeding and subsequent risk of atopic eczema', *Arch Dis Child* (1985) **60:** pp. 722–6.

17. Soothill JF, Stokes CR, Turner MW, Norman AP, Taylor B, 'Predisposing factors and the development of reagenic allergy in infancy', *Clin All* (1976) **61:** pp. 305–19.

18. Williams HE, McNichol KN, 'Prevalence, natural history and relationship of wheezy bronchitis and asthma in children. An epidemiological study', *Br Med J* (1969) **4:** pp. 321–5.

19. Williams HE, Phelan PD, 'The natural history of childhood asthma through adolescence', *Australian Paed J* (1977) **13:** pp. 88–90.

20. Martin AJ, McLennan LA, Landau LI, Phelan PD, 'The natural history of childhood asthma to adult life', *Br Med J* (1980) **280:** pp. 1397–1400.

Chapter 2

1. Wharton J, Polak JM, Bloom SR, Will JA, Brown MR, Pearce AGF, 'Substance P-like immunoreactive nerves in mammalian lung', *Invest Cell Pathol* (1979) **2:** pp. 3–10.

2. Chai H, Farr RS, Froehlich Mathison DA, McLean JA, 'Standardization of bronchial inhalation challenge procedure', *J All Clin Immunol* (1975) **56:** pp. 323–37.

3. Murray AB, Ferguson AC, Morrison B, 'Airways responsiveness to histamine as a test for overall severity of asthma in children', *J All Clin Immunol* (1981) **68:** pp. 119–24.

4. Silverman M, Anderson SD, 'Standardization of exercise tests in asthmatic children', *Arch Dis Child* (1972) **47:** pp. 882–9.

5. Godfrey S, Konig P, 'Inhibition of exercise-induced asthma by different pharmacological pathways', *Thorax* (1976) **31:** pp. 137–43.

6. Anderson SD, Connolly W, Godfrey S, 'Comparisons of bronchoconstriction induced by cycling and running', *Thorax* (1971) **26:** pp. 369–401.

7. Deal EC, McFadden ER, Ingram RH, Strauss RH, Jaeger JJ, 'Role of respiratory heat exchange in production of exercise-induced asthma', *J Appl Physiol* (1979) **46:** pp. 467–75.

8. Deal EC, McFadden ER, Ingram RH, Jaeger JJ, 'Esophageal temperature during exercise in asthmatic and non-asthmatic subjects', *J Appl Physiol* (1979) **46:** pp. 484–90.

9. Hahn A, Anderson SA, Morton AR, Black JL, Fitch KY, 'A reinterpretation of the effect of temperature and water content of the inspired air in exercised-induced asthma', *Am Rev Respir Dis* (1984) **130**: pp. 575–9.

10. Edmunds AT, Tooley M, Godfrey S, 'The refractory period after exercise-induced asthma, its duration and relation to severity of exercise', *Am Rev Respir Dis* (1978) **117**: pp. 247–54.

11. Wilson N, Barnes PJ, Vickers H, Silverman M, 'Hyperventilation induced asthma: evidence for two mechanisms', *Thorax* (1982) **37**: pp. 657–62.

12. Galder-Sebaldt M, McLaughlin FJ, Levison H, 'Comparison of cold air, ultrasonic mist and methacholine inhalations as a test of bronchial reactivity in normal and asthmatic children', *J Pediatrics* (1985) **107**: pp. 526–30.

13. Vargaftig BB, Lefort J, Chignard M, Ben Veniste J, 'Platelet-activating factor induces a platelet dependent bronchoconstriction unrelated to the formation of prostaglandin derivatives', *European J Pharmacol* (1980) **65**: pp. 185–92.

14. Warner JO, Price JF, Soothill JF, Hey EN, 'Controlled trial of hyposensitisation to *Dermatophagoides pteronyssinus* in children with asthma', *Lancet* (1978) **ii**: pp. 912–15.

15. Cockcroft DW, 'Mechanism of perennial allergic asthma', *Lancet* (1983) **ii**: pp. 253–6.

Chapter 3

1. Nairn JR, Bennett AJ, Andrew, JD, MacArthur P, 'A study of respiratory function in normal schoolchildren; the peak flow rate', *Arch Dis Child* (1961) **36**: pp. 253–6.

2. Cogswell JJ, Hull D, Milner AD, Norman AP, Taylor B, 'Lung function in childhood I. The forced expiratory volumes in healthy children using a spirometer and reverse plethysmograph', *Br J Dis Chest* (1975) **69**: pp. 40–8.

3. Cogswell JJ, Hull D, Milner AD, Norman AP, Taylor B, 'Lung function in childhood III. Measurement of air flow resistance in healthy children', *Br J Dis Chest* (1975) **69**: pp. 177–87.

4. Zapletal A, Motoxama EK, Van de Woestijne KP, Hunt VR, Bouhuys A, 'Maximum expiratory flow volume curves and airways conductance in children and adolescents', *J Appl Physiol* (1969) **26**: pp. 308–16.

5. DuBois AB, Bothello SY, Bedell GN, Marshall R, Comroe JH, 'Rapid plethysmographic method for measuring thoracic gas volume; comparison with a nitrogen wash-out method for measuring FRC in normal subjects', *J Clin Invest* (1956) **35**: pp. 322–6.

6. Shore S, Milic-Emili J, Martin JG, 'Assessment of body plethysmographic techniques for the measurement of thoracic gas volume', *Am Rev Respir Dis* (1982) **126**: pp. 515–20.

7. DuBois AB, Bothello SY, Comrie JH. 'A new method for measuring airways resistance in man using a body plethysmograph: values in normal subjects and in patients with respiratory disease', *J Clin Invest* (1956) **35**: pp. 327–30.

8. Zapletal A, Samanek M, Pavl T, 'Upstream and total airways conductance in children and adolescents', *Bull Europ Physiopathology Resp* (1982) **18**: pp. 31–7.

9. Cogswell JJ, Hull D, Milner AD, Norman AP, Taylor B, 'Lung function in childhood II. Thoracic gas volumes and helium functional residual capacity measurements in healthy children', *Br J Dis Chest* (1975) **69**: pp. 118–124.

10. Morse M, Schlutz FW, Cassels DE, 'The lung volume and its subdivisions in normal boys 10-17 years of age', *J Clin Invest* (1952) **31**: pp. 380–91.

11. Milner AD, Ingram D, 'PEFRs in children under 5 years of age', *Arch Dis Child* (1970) **45**: pp. 820–3.

12. Cogswell JJ, 'Forced oscillation technique for determination of resistance to breathing in children', *Arch Dis Child* (1973) **48**: pp. 259–66.

13. Greenough A, Stocks J, Helms P, 'Functional residual capacity and total respiratory compliance in young children', *Pediatric Pulmonology* (1986) **2**: pp. 321–6.

14. Rutter N, Milner AD, Hiller EJ, 'Effect of bronchodilator on respiratory resistance in infants and young children with bronchiolitis and wheezy bronchitis', *Arch Dis Child* (1975) **50**: pp. 719–22.

15. Helms P, 'Problems with plethysmographic estimation of lung volume in infants and young children', *J Appl Physiol* (1982) **53**: pp. 698–702.

16. Stocks J, Levy NM, Godfrey S, 'A new apparatus for the accurate measurement of airways resistance in infancy', *J Appl Physiol* (1977) **43**: pp. 155–9.

17. Taussig LM, Landau LI, Godfrey S, Arad I, 'Determinants of forced expiratory flow in newborn infants', *J Appl Physiol* (1982) **53**: pp. 1220–7.

18. Hoskyns EW, Milner AD, Hopkin IE, 'Validity of the forced expiratory flow volume loops in the neonatal period', *Am Rev Respir Dis* (1986) Submitted.

Chapter 4

1. Lee DA, Winslow NR, Speight A, Hey EN, 'Prevalence and spectrum of asthma in childhood', *Br Med J* (1983) **286**: pp. 1256–8.

2. Wilmott RW, Chapter 10—'Allergy and infection in cystic fibrosis', In *Neonatal and Paediatric Respiratory Medicine* (Eds AD Milner and R Martin, Butterworths, London 1985).

3. Laughlin JJ, Eigen H, 'Pulmonary function abnormality in survivors of near drowning', *J Pediatrics* (1982) **100**: pp. 26–30.

4. Webb MSC, Henry RL, Milner AD, Stokes GM, Swarbrick AS, 'Continuing respiratory problems three and a half years after acute viral bronchiolitis', *Arch Dis Child* (1985) **60**: pp. 1064–7.

5.   Mok JYQ, Waugh PR, Simpson H, 'Mycoplasma pneumoniae infection—A follow-up study of fifty children with respiratory illness', *Arch Dis Child* (1979) **54:** pp. 506–11.

6.   Johnston IDA, Anderson HR, Lambert HP, Patel S, 'Respiratory morbidity and lung function after whooping cough', *Lancet* (1983) **ii:** pp. 1104–8.

7.   Taylor B, Norman AP, Orgel HA, Stokes CR, Turner MW, Soothill JF, 'Transient IgA deficiency and pathogenesis of infantile atopy', *Lancet* (1973) **ii:** pp. 111–13.

8.   Adkinson NF, 'The radioallergosorbent test: uses and abuses', *J All Clin Immunol* (1980) **65:** pp. 1–5.

9.   Aas K, 'The diagnosis of hypersensitivity to ingested foods, Reliability of skin prick tests and the radioallergosorbent test with different materials', *Clin All* (1978) **8:** pp. 39–43.

10. Price JF, Turner MW, Warner JO, Soothill JF, 'Immunological studies in asthmatic children undergoing antigen challenge in the skin, lungs and nose', *Clin All* (1983) **13:** pp. 419–28.

11. Speight A, Lee DA, Hey EN, 'Underdiagnosis and undertreatment of asthma in childhood', *Br Med J* (1983) **286:** pp. 1253–6.

Chapter 5

1.   William HE, McNichol KN, 'Prevalence, natural history and relationship of wheezy bronchitis in children. An epidemiological study', *Br Med J* (1969) **4:** pp. 321–5.

2.   Cockcroft DW, 'Mechanism of perennial allergic asthma', *Lancet* (1983) **ii:** pp. 253–6.

3.   Turpeinen M, Kuokkanen J, Backman A, 'Adrenaline and nebulized salbutamol in acute asthma', *Arch Dis Child* (1984) **59:** pp. 666–8.

4.   Anderson SD, Seale JP, Rozea P, Bandler J, Theobald G, Lindsay DA, 'Inhaled and oral salbutamol in exercise-induced asthma', *Am Rev Respir Dis* (1976) **114:** pp. 493–500.

5.   Clay MM, Pavia D, Newman SP, Leonnard-Jones T, Clarke SW, 'Assessment of jet nebulizers for lung aerosol therapy', *Lancet* (1983) **ii:** pp. 592–4.

6.   Henry RL, Milner AD, Davies JG, 'Simple drug delivery system for use by young asthmatics', *Br Med J* (1983) **286:** pp. 2021–2.

7.   Lenney W, Milner AD, Hiller EJ, 'Continuous and intermittent salbutamol tablet administration in asthmatic children', *Br J Dis Chest* (1979) **73:** pp. 277–81.

8.   Weinberger M, Hendeles L, 'Chapter 14—Use of theophylline for asthma', In *Asthma* 2nd ed (Eds TJH Clark and S Godfrey, Chapman and Hall, London   1983).

9.   Edmunds AT, Carswell F, Robinson P, Hughes AO, 'Controlled trial of cromoglycate and slow release aminophylline in perennial childhood asthma', *Br Med J* (1980) **281:** p. 842.

10. Elias-Jones AC, Higenbottam TW, Barnes WP, Godden DJ, 'Sustained release theophylline in nocturnal asthma', *Arch Dis Child* (1984) **59:** pp. 1159–61.

11. Groggins RC, Hiller EJ, Milner AD, Stokes GM, 'Ketotifen in the prophylaxis of childhood asthma', *Arch Dis Child* (1981) **56:** pp. 304–5.

12. Silverman M, Connelly W, Balfour-Lynn L, Godfrey S, 'Longterm trial of disodium cromoglycate and isoprenaline in children with asthma', *Br Med J* (1972) **3:** pp. 378–81.

13. Balfour-Lynn L, Tooley M, Godfrey S, 'Relationship of exercise-induced asthma to clinical asthma in childhood', *Arch Dis Child* (1981) **56:** pp. 450–4.

14. Bar-Yishay E, Gur I, Levy M, Volozni D, Godfrey S, 'Duration of action of sodium cromoglycate on exercise-induced asthma: comparison of 2 formulations', *Arch Dis Child* (1983) **58:** pp. 624–7.

15. Godfrey S, Balfour Lynn L, Tooley M, 'A three to five year follow-up of the use of aerosol beclomethasone dipropionate in childhood asthma', *J All Clin Immunol* (1978) **62:** pp. 335–9.

16. Field HV, Jenkinson PMA, Frame MH, Warner JO, 'Asthma treatment with a new corticosteroid aerosol budesonide administered twice daily by a spacer inhaler', *Arch Dis Child* (1982) **57:** pp. 864–6.

17. Brogden RN, 'Chapter 8—Inhaled steroids: pharmacology and toxicology' In *Steroids in Asthma* (Ed. TJH Clark. Adis Press, Sydney 1983).

18. Wyatt R, Waschek J, Weinberger M, Sherman B, 'Effects of inhaled beclomethasone dipropionate and alternate day prednisolone on pituitary adrenal function in children with chronic asthma', *N Eng J Med* (1978) **299:** pp. 1387–90.

19. J. Warner—personal communication.

20. Hiller EJ, Milner AD, 'Betamethasone 17 valerate and disodium cromoglycate in severe childhood asthma', *Br J Dis Chest* (1975) **69:** pp. 103–6.

21. Hodges IGC, Milner AD, Stokes GM, 'Bronchodilator effect of two inhaled H_1 receptor antagonists, clemastine and chlorpheniramine in wheezy schoolchildren', *Br J Dis Chest* (1982) **77:** pp. 270–5.

22. Henry RL, Hodges IGC, Milner AD, Stokes GM, 'Bronchodilator effects of the H_1 receptor antagonist–clemastine', *Arch Dis Child* (1983) **58:** pp. 304–5.

23. Wichert P, 'Ketotifen, an anti-allergic drug: Pharmacological figures and clinical experience', *Prog Respir Res* (1980) **14:** p. 181.

24. Lenney W, 'Nebulized salbutamol in treatment of acute asthma in children', *Lancet* (1978) **i:** pp. 440–1.

25. Hendeles L, Weinberger ML, Johnson G. Theophylline, In *Applied Pharmacokinetics* (Eds WE Evans JJ Schentag   Applied Therapeutics Inc, San Francisco 1980).

26. Coswell JJ, Simpkiss MJ, 'Nebulized sodium cromoglycate in recurrently wheezy preschool children', *Arch Dis Child* (1985) **60:** pp. 736–8.

27. Storr J, Lenney CA, Lenney W, 'Nebulized beclomethasone dipropionate in preschool asthma', *Arch Dis Child* (1986) **61:** pp. 270–3.

28. Webb MSC, Milner AD, Hiller EJ, Henry RL, 'Nebulized beclomethasone dipropionate suspension', *Arch Dis Child* (1986) In press.

29. Lenney W, Milner AD, 'At what age do bronchodilators work?' *Arch Dis Child* (1978) **53:** pp. 532–5.

30. Prenderville A, Green S, Silverman M, 'Bronchial responsiveness to histamine in wheezing infants', *Thorax* (1986) In press.

31. Prenderville A, Green S, Silverman M, 'Airways responsiveness in wheezy infants. Evidence for functional beta adrenergic receptors', *Thorax* (1986) In press.

32. Hodges IGC, Groggins RC, Milner AD, Stokes GM, 'Bronchodilator effects of inhaled ipratropium bromide in wheezy toddlers', *Arch Dis Child* (1981) **56:** pp. 729–32.

33. Henry RL, Hiller EJ, Milner AD, Hodges IGC, Stokes GM, 'Nebulized ipratropium bromide and sodium cromoglycate in the first 2 years of life', *Arch Dis Child* (1984) **59:** pp. 54–7.

34. Geller-Bernstein C, Levin S, 'Nebulized sodium cromoglycate in the treatment of wheezy bronchitis in infants and young children', *Respiration* (1982) **43:** pp. 294–8.

35. Tal A, Bavilski C, Yohai D, Bearman JE, Gorodischer R, Moses SW, 'Dexamethasone and salbutamol in the treatment of bronchiolitis', *J Pediatrics* (1983) **71:** pp. 13–18.

36. Webb MSC, Henry RL, Milner AD, 'Oral corticosteroids for wheezing attacks under 18 months', *Arch Dis Child* (1986) **61:** pp. 15–19.

Chapter 6

1. Webb MSC, Henry RL, Milner AD, Stokes GM, Swarbrick AS, 'Continuing respiratory problems three and a half years after acute viral bronchiolitis', *Arch Dis Child* (1985) **60:** pp. 1064–7.

2. Russell G, Jones SP, 'Selection of skin tests in childhood asthma', *Br J Dis Chest* (1976) **70:** pp. 104–6.

3. May CD, Bock SA, 'A modern clinical approach to hypersensitivity', *Allergy* (1978) **33:** pp. 167–71.

4. Wilson WM, Silverman M, 'The diagnosis of food sensitivity in childhood asthma', *J R Soc Med* (1985) **Suppl. 5:** pp. 11–16.

5. Lichtenstein LM, 'An evaluation of the role of immunotherapy in asthma', *Ann Rev Respir Dis* (1978) **61:** p. 268.

6. Warner JO, Price JF, Soothill JF, Hey EN, 'Controlled trial of hyposensitization to *Dermatophagoides pteronyssinus* in children with asthma', *Lancet* (1978) **ii:** pp. 912–15.

7. Price JF, Warner JO, Hey EN, Turner MW, Soothill JF, 'A controlled trial of hypersensitization with adsorbed *Dermatophagoides pteronyssinus* antigen in childhood asthma: in vivo aspects', *Clin All* (1984) **14:** pp. 209–19.

8. Vervloet D, Khairallah FC, Arnand D, Charpin J, 'A prospective study of the safety of immunotherapy', *Clin All* (1980) **10:** p. 59.

Chapter 7

1. Dunnill MS, Massarella GR, Anderson J, 'A comparison of the quantitative anatomy of the bronchi in normal subjects, in status asthmaticus, in chronic bronchitis and emphysema', *Thorax* (1969) **24:** pp. 176–9.

2. Mitchell RG, Dawson B, 'Educational and social characteristics in children with asthma', *Arch Dis Child* (1973) **48:** pp. 467–71.

Chapter 8

1. Chu SS, Pearce SJ, 'Acupuncture point stimulation in bronchial asthma', *Thorax* (1976) **31:** pp. 428–32.

2. Nagarathna R, Nagendra HR, 'Yoga for bronchial asthma: a controlled study', *Br Med J* (1985) **291:** pp. 1077–9.

3. Ben-Dov I, Amirav I, Shochina M, Amitai I, Bar-Yishay C, Godfrey S, 'Effect of negative ionization of inspired air on the response of asthmatic children to exercise and inhaled histamine', *Thorax* (1983) **38:** pp. 584–8.

Chapter 9

1. Jones RS, Buston MH, Wharton MJ, 'The effect of exercise on ventilatory function in the child with asthma', *Br J Dis Chest* (1962) **56:** pp. 78–86.

2. Schnall RP, Landau LI, 'The protective effects of short sprints on exercise-induced asthma', *Thorax* (1980) **35:** pp. 828–32.

3. Graff-Lonnevig V, Bevegard S, Eriksson BO, 'Two year follow-up of asthmatic boys participating in a physical activity programme', *Acta Paed Scand* (1980) **69:** pp. 347–52.

4. Jones RS, Wharton MJ, Buston MH, 'The place of physical exercise and bronchodilator drugs in the assessment of the asthmatic child', *Arch Dis Child* (1963) **38:** pp. 539–45.

5. Francis PWJ, Krastins IRB, Levison H, 'Oral and inhaled salbutamol in the prevention of exercise-induced bronchospasm', *J Pediatrics* (1980) **66:** pp. 103–8.

6. Davies SE, 'The effects of disodium cromoglycate on exercise-induced asthma', *Br Med J* (1968) **3:** pp. 593–4.

7. McNeill RS, Nairn JR, Millar JS, Ingrams CG, 'Exercise-induced asthma', *Q J Med* (1966) **35:** pp. 55–67.

8. Henriksen JM 'The effect of inhaled corticosteroids on exercise-induced asthma: randomised double blind crossover study of budesonide in asthmatic children', *Br Med J* (1985) **291:** pp. 248–9.

9. Barnes PJ, Levy J, 'Nocturnal asthma', *Royal Society of Medicine International Congress and Symposium series* (1984) London UK.

10. Fairfax AJ, McNabb WR, Davies HJ, Spiro SG, 'Slow release oral salbutamol and aminophylline in nocturnal asthma', *Thorax* (1980) **35:** pp. 526–9.

Chapter 10

1. McKenzie SA, Edmunds AT, Godfrey S, 'Status asthmaticus in children: a one year study', *Arch Dis Child* (1979) **54:** pp. 561–6.

2. Edmunds AT, Godfrey S, 'Cardiovascular response during acute severe asthma and its treatment in children', *Thorax* (1981) **35:** pp. 745–50.

3. Beck R, Robertson C, Galdes-Sebaldt M, Levison H, 'Combined salbutamol and ipratropium bromide by inhalation in the treatment of severe acute asthma', *J Pediatrics* (1985) **107:** pp. 605–8.

4. Stalcup SA, Mellins RB, 'Mechanical forces producing pulmonary edema in asthma', *N Eng J Med* (1977) **297:** pp. 592–6.

Chapter 11

1. Speight A, Lee DA, Hey EN, 'Underdiagnosis and undertreatment of asthma in childhood', *Br Med J* (1983) **286:** pp. 1253–6.

2. Marks BE, Hillier VF, 'General practitioners' views on asthma in childhood', *Br Med J* (1983) **287:** pp. 949–51.

3. Toop LJ, 'Active approach to recognizing asthma in general practice', *Br Med J* (1985) **290:** pp. 1629–31.

4. Lee DA, Winslow NR, Speight A, Hey EN, 'Prevalence and spectrum of asthma in childhood', *Br Med J* (1983) **286:** pp. 1256–8.

5. Anderson HR, Bailey PA, Cooper JS, Palmer JC, 'Influence of morbidity, illness label, and social, family and health service factors on drug treatment of childhood asthma', *Lancet* (1981) **ii:** pp. 1030–2.

6. Levy M, Parmar M, Coetzee D, Duffy SW, 'Respiratory consultations in asthmatic compared to non-asthmatic children in general practice', *Br Med J* (1985) **291:** pp. 29–30.

7. Frew AJ, Macfarlane JT, 'Poor inhaler technique may be perpetuated by clinical staff', *Practitioner* (1984) **228:** p. 883.

8. Jenkinson D, 'Use of a nebulizer for acute asthma', *J R Coll Gen Pract* (1983) **33:** p. 725.

9. Pearce JL, Wesley HMM, 'Children with asthma: will nebulized salbutamol reduce hospital admissions?' *Br Med J* (1985) **290:** pp. 595–7.

10. Barritt P, 'The use of nebulizer systems in asthma. Editorial' *J R Coll Gen Pract* (1985) **35:** p. 171.

11. Laroche CM, Harries AVK, Newton RCF, Britton MG, 'Domiciliary nebulizers in asthma: a district survey', *Br Med J* (1985) **290:** pp. 1611–13.

12. Freelander M, Van Asperen PP, 'Nebuhaler versus nebulizer in children with acute asthma', *Br Med J* (1984) **288:** pp. 1873–4.

13. Henry RL, Milner AD, Davies JG, 'Simple drug delivery system for use by young asthmatics', *Br Med J* (1983) **286:** p. 2021.

14. Lee J, Evans HE, 'Aerosol bag for administration of bronchodilators to young asthmatic children', *J Pediatrics* (1984) **73,2:** pp. 230–2.

15. Pendleton D, Schofeld T, Tate P, Havelock P, *The consultation. An approach to learning and teaching* (Oxford University Press, Oxford   1984).

16. Modell M, Harding JM, Horder EJ, Williams PR, 'Improving the care of asthmatic patients in general practice', *Br Med J* (1983) **286:** pp. 2027–30.

17. Hilton S, Sibbald B, Anderson HR, Freeling P, 'Controlled evaluation of the effects of patient education on asthma morbidity in general practice', *Lancet* (1986) **i:** pp. 26–9.

18. Harding JM, Modell M, 'How patients manage asthma', *J R Coll Gen Pract* (1985) **35:** pp. 226–8.

19. Anderson HR, Bailey P, West S, 'Trends in the hospital care of acute childhood asthma 1970-78: a regional study', *Br Med J* (1980) **281:** pp. 1191–4.

20. Johnson AJ, Nunn AJ, Somner AR, Stableforth DE, Stewart CJ, 'Circumstances of death from asthma', *Br Med J* (1984) **288:** pp. 1870–2.

21. Pearson R, 'Asthma care' *Update* (1986) 15 June: pp. 1139–47.

22. Hart JT, 'Wheezing in young children: problems of measurement and management', *J R Coll Gen Pract* (1986) **36:** pp. 78–81.

Sources

Lee D et al, *Br Med J* (1983) **285** for Figure 1.1; Silverman M, *Asthma in Childhood* (Current Medical Literature Ltd, 1985) for Figure 1.2; Stocks J, *J Appl Physio* (1977) **43** for Figure 2.1; Henricksen J, *Br Med J* (1985) **291** for Figure 2.4; Milner A D, *Pharm Ther* (1982) **17** for Figure 4.4; Grimwood H et al, *Arch Dis Child* (1983) **58** for Figure 5.2; Henry R et al, *Br Med J* (1983) **286** for Figure 5.7; Groggins R et al, *Arch Dis Child* (1980) **55** for Figures 5.9 and 5.11; Lenney W and Milner A D, *Arch Dis Child* (1981) **56** for Figure 5.12; Hodges I et al, *Arch Dis Child* (1981) **56** for Figure 5.13; Weiler-Ravell D and Godfrey S, *J All* (1981) **67** for Figure 9.1; Clark T J H and Godfrey S, *Asthma* 2nd edition (Chapman and Hall, 1983) for Figure 10.5.

Index

Page numbers in *italic* refers to the
   illustrations

acetylcholine, 7
acupuncture, 86
acute attacks: management, 94–108, 112–13
  steriod treatment, 58, 107–8
Addison's disease, 38
adenoviral infections, 94
adolescents, 115
adrenal glands, 56, 58
adrenaline, 8, 45
Aerochamber, 48, *50*, 60, 63, 100
aerosol therapy, 46–8, 49, *50–1*, 60, 100,
  110, 130–1
Aerospacer, 48, 56
air: humidity, 11, 80–1, 104–5, *105*
  temperature, 11–12, 42, 90
airways: diameter, 7–8
  lung function tests, 18–30
  resistance test, 23–5
  site of bronchoconstriction, 13–14, *15*
allergic rhinitis, 41
allergies, 4–5, 31, 39
  acute attacks, 95
  allergen avoidance, 69–75
  allergen challenge, 12–14
  allergen bronchial provocation, 42
  conjunctival provocation, 41
  desensitization, 75–7, 117
  skin tests, 39–41, *40–41*, 69, 70, 72
    antitrypsin deficiency, 58
alternative therapies, 85–7, 117
alveoli, diameter, 7
alveolitis, fibrosing, 36
aminophylline: in acute attacks, 101, *101*,
  102, 105, 108
  dosage, 53
  and mechanical ventilation, 107
  side-effects, 54, 96
Anderson, Sandy, 11
animal furs, allergy, 40, 69
antibiotics, 93, 98
antihistamines, 59
appearance, acute attacks, 95

arachidonic acid, 56
arterial blood gases, 99, 102, 103, 107
asthma: allergies, 69–77
  alternative therapies, 85–7, 117
  bronchiectasis and, 92–3
  chronic, 113–19
  asthma clinics, 117
  definition, 1–2
  diagnosis, 31–42, 94–102, 109–10
  drug treatment, 43–68
  exercise-induced bronchoconstriction,
    88–9, *90*
  incidence, 2–3
  investigations, 9–14, 18–30, 36–42, 99
  management of, 78–84
  management of acute attacks, 94–108,
    112–13
  management in general practice, 109–19
  nocturnal, 52, 61, 81, 90–2
  review procedures, 117–18
Asthma Society, 44, 112, 113
auscultation, 35–6, 98
autonomic nervous system, 7, *9*
autosuggestion, 87

babies: bronchiolitis, 4
  lung function tests, 28–30
  obstetric and birth history, 33
  oxygen therapy, 103
beclomethasone dipropionate, 56, 57, 59,
  63, 67
Becotide, 131
bedding, 69, 71, 72
bedwetting, 92
Berotec, 131
beta$_2$ blocking agents, 7
beta$_2$ stimulants, 7, 45
  acute attacks, 100–1, 107
  aerosol devices, 46–7
  bronchiectasis, 93
  exercise-induced bronchoconstriction,
    10, 89

beta₂ stimulants (*cont.*)
frequency of use, 51
lung collapse, 92
lung function tests, 36–8
and mechanical ventilation, 107
nebulizer compressor system, 48, *100*
nocturnal asthma, 90–2
peak flow rates, *37*
and physiotherapy, 104
used with sodium cromoglycate, 54, 62–3
used with steriods, 57, 58, 59
used with theophylline therapy, 52
for younger children, 59, 61, 65, 67
betamethasone valerate, 57
birth history, 33
blood gases, 16–17, *16*, 99, 102, 103, 107
blood tests, 38
Boyle's law, 23–25
brachial artery, 99
breathing exercises, 79–80, 86
breathing rates, acute attacks, 98
breathlessness, 31
Bricanyl, 130
bronchial lavage, 107
bronchial plugging, 33
bronchial provocation, 42
bronchiectasis, 31, 32, 33, 58, 92–3
bronchioles, diameter, 7
bronchiolitis, 1, 4, 32, 33, 35, 58, 94, 110
bronchitis, 32, 109
bronchoconstriction, 7–17
and blood gases, 16–17, *16*
exercise-induced, 88–9, *90*
in healthy lungs, 7–8
mechanisms of, 9–13
site of, 13–16, *15*
bronchodilatation, 7
bronchodilators: in general practice, 110–11
inhalation therapy, 51, 59–60, 111–12,
130–1
oral therapy, 48, 59
selection of devices, 46–8
slow-release preparations, 52
tachycardia, 96
for younger children, 59–60
bronchomalacia, 32, 94
bronchopulmonary aspergillosis, 38
bronchopulmonary dysplasia, 94
bronchoscopy, 92, 95
budesonide, *11*, 57, 63

caffeine, 85
candida, 56
cannulae, oxygen therapy, 102, *103*
carbachol, 9, 65
carbon dioxide, *15*, 17, 102
cardiac arrest, 107
cardiac decompensation, 53
case histories, 120–8
cat fur, 69
catecholamines, 7, 10

cerebral palsy, 35
Chai technique, 9
chemotactic chemicals, 12, 13
chest deformity, 33, 34, *36*, 80
chest x-rays, 92, 94, 95, 99
cholestatic jaundice, 53
cholinergic blocking agents, 10
chronic asthma, management of, 113–19
cilia: abnormalities, 92
activity, 8
immotile cilia syndrome, 31
cimetidine, 53
clemastine, 59
clinical assessment, 33–6
clinics, 117
clubbing, 33
coffee cup delivery system, 48, *50*, *51*, 60,
65, 66, 100
cold air, and bronchoconstriction, 11–12, 42
colds, 48
compression, dynamic, 13–15
congenital lobar emphysema, 94
conjunctival provocation, 41
conjunctivitis, 41
cor pulmonale, 53
corticosteroids, 13, 91
coughing, 31, 32, 110
crepitations, 35, 94, 98
croup, 94
cyanosis, 34, 95, 99
cystic fibrosis, 1, 31, 32, 58

dairy products, 74, 117
death, 5–6
dehydration, 104
dermatitis herpetiformis, 38
desensitization, allergies, 75–7, 117
diagnosis, 31–42, 94–102, 109–10
diaries, symptom, 118
diarrhoea, 73–4
diets, exclusion, 74–5, 117
see also food allergy
discharge letters, 116
disease index, 118
distilled water, ultrasonically nebulized,
12, 42
diurnal variations, 91
doctor: relations with hospitals, 115–17
relations with parents, 113–14
relations with patients, 114–15
dosage: steroids, 57
theophylline, 52–4
drowning, 31
drugs, 43–68
bronchodilators, 45–9, 59–61
exercise-induced bronchoconstriction, 89
in general practice, 110–12
inhalation therapy, 45–6, 51, 59–60,
110–11, 130–1
oral therapy, 45–6, 48–52, 59

drugs (*cont.*)
    selection of devices, 46–8
    see also individual drugs
dry spirometers, 20
dynamic compression, 13–16
dysphonia, 56

ECG monitoring, 101, 102, 107
eczema, 4, 38, 69
education, patient, 44
emotional stress, 80, 83, 95
Empey, DW, 4
emphysema, congenital lobar, 94
endotracheal tubes, 106, 107
environmental factors, 4, 5
eosinophilia, 38
eosinophilia leukaemia, 38
eosinophils, 12, 13, 38, 56, 92
ephedrine, 45
epithelium, damage, 8
erythromycin, 53
exclusion diets, 74–5, 117
exercise, asthma investigations, 10–11, *11*,
    36, 42
exercise-induced bronchoconstriction (EIB),
    88–9, *90*

face masks, oxygen therapy, 103
family history, 33
fenoterol, 46, *47*, 61
fibrosing alveolitis, 36
flow volume curves, 22–3, 29–30, *30*, 38
food allergy, 39–41, 72–5, 95, 117
foot-pump nebulizers, 81, *83*
forced expiratory volume (FEV), 20–2, *21*, 23
forced oscillation technique, 27, *27*
foreign bodies, inhaled, 31, 32, 33, 94, 95,
    96, 97
functional residual capacity, 28
fungal infections, 93
fungal spores, allergy, 95
furs, allergy, 40, 69

gamma camera ventilation/perfusion
    studies, 95
gas dilution technique, 26
general practice, management of asthma
    in, 109–19
genetics, 1, 3–4
growth, 38, *34*, *35*, 118
growth hormones, 33, 56

H type tracheo-oesophageal fistula, 94
haemoglobin, 17
Haemophilus influenzae, 92
Hahnemann, Samuel, 86

Halermatic, 54, 62
hand tremor, 48
Harrison sulci, 34, 80, *81*
hay fever, 4, 59, 69, 70, 82, 88
head boxes, oxygen therapy, 103
health visitors, 118–19
heart failure, 94, 107
heart rate, acute attacks, 96–8
hepatitis, 53
herbal remedies, 85
heroin, 85
histamine, 11, 65
    and fizzy drinks, 72, *73*
    histamine challenge, 9, *10*, 11, 12, 36, 42
    skin tests, 40
history, 32–3, 40
holidays, 82–3
homeopathy, 86
hormones, 8, 33, 56
Hospital for Sick Children, London, 76
hospitals: emergencies, 115–16
    referral to, 116–17
house dust, 12, 40, 69, 70, 71
house dust mite, 12, 40, 69, 70, 71, 76, 81,
    83, 91
housing, 81–2
humidity, 11, 80–1, 104–5, *105*
hydration, 104–5, *105*
hydrocortisone, 101, 102, 105, 107, 108
hyperinflation, 13, 16, 35, 58, 94, 98, *123*
hyperventilation, 17, 95
hypnosis, 87
hypothalamus, 56
hypoxia, 95, 102
hysterical hyperventilation, 95

immotile cilia syndrome, 31
immunization, 5
immunoglobulin levels, 38
infants *see* babies
infections, 53
influenza, 1, 4
inhalation therapy, 45–6, 51, 59–60, 110–
    11, 130–1
Intal, 131
intubation, 106
ions, negative, 87
ipratropium bromide, 61, *62*, 65–6, *66*, 67,
    89, 102
isoprenaline, 45, 102

jaundice, cholestatic, 53

ketotifen, 54, 59
klebsiella, 92

laryngeal/tracheal stenosis, 32
laryngotracheobronchitis, 94

late response, 12–13, 45
leukaemia, eosinophilia, 38
leukotrienes, 12, 56
lipomodulin, 55
liver: and hyperinflation, 35
    physical examination, 98
lobar collapse, 33, 99
lobectomy, 92
Loeffler's syndrome, 92
lungs: bronchoconstriction, 7–17
    clearance of secretions, 78
    collapse, 33, 78, 79, 92, 98, 99, 124
    lung function tests, 18–30, 36–8, 99
    site of bronchoconstriction, 13, 15
lymphocytes, 67

macrocortin, 55
mast cells, 8, 11, 12, 13, 54, 59
maximum mid-expiratory flow (MMEF), 21–
    2, 22
measles, 33
mechanical ventilation, 106–7
mediastinal tumours, 32
methacholine challenge, 9, 11, 42
milk allergy, 5, 41, 74
milk aspiration, 32, 94
mist tents, 104–5
morphine, 85
mortality rates, 5–6
moulds, allergy, 70
mucosal oedema, 8
muscles: airways diameter, 7–8
    constriction, 8
    physiotherapy, 78
Mycoplasma pneumoniae, 1, 4, 33
mystatin, 56

nasal provocation, 41
nasoendotracheal tubes, 106
Nebuhaler, 48, 50, 56, 60, 100
nebulizers, 48, 60, 62, 63, 82, 83, 100, 102,
    111–12
negative-ion generators, 87
nervous system, 7
    autonomic, 7, 9
    parasympathetic, 7, 9
    sympathetic, 7
neural reflexes, 8
neuromuscular disorders, 35
neutrophil chemotactic factor, 11
neutrophils, 12, 13, 56, 92
nitrogen, gas dilution technique, 26
nocturnal asthma, 52, 61, 81, 90–2
non-adrenergic inhibitory system, 7
nurses, 118–19

obliterative bronchiolitis, 36, 58
obstetric history, 33

oedema, 40, 105
oesophageal balloon, 28, 29
oesophagus, total pulmonary resistance,
    28, 29
opium, 85
oral therapy, 45–6, 48–51, 59
oxygen, in blood, 16, 17
oxygen therapy, 95, 102, 103,104
oxyhaemoglobin, 17

palpation, 98
pancuronium, 107
panic, 79–80
paralysis, mechanical ventilation, 107
parasympathetic nervous system, 7, 9
parents, 113–14, 115–16
partial expiratory flow volume curves, 30,
    30
partial flow volume curves, 23
patients: education, 44
    records, 118
    relations with doctors, 114–15
peak expiratory flow rate (PEFR), 18–19, 19,
    20, 23
peak flow meters, 9, 18, 19, 26, 36–38, 99,
    99, 112
percussion, 98
phosphodiesterase, 52
physiotherapy, 78–80, 92, 104
pirbuterol, 46, 61
pituitary gland, 56
placebo reaction, 80
platelet-activating factor, 12, 13
plethysmography, 23–25, 24, 25, 26, 28, 38,
    58
plugging, airways, 33, 104
pneumococci, 92
pneumonia, 94
pneumotachographs, 20, 22–3, 24, 27,
    28–30
pneumothorax, 95, 98, 99
pollen: allergy, 12, 40, 69, 70, 95
    desensitization, 76
polycythaemia, 38
powder delivery systems, 46, 47, 48, 59,
    63–4, 130–1
prednisolone, 58, 64, 107, 112
    allergen bronchial provocation, 42
    diagnostic therapy, 110
    and growth rates, 34, 35
    lung function tests, 38, 39
premature babies, 33
prostaglandins, 12, 56
pseudomonas, 92
psychotherapy, 80
Pulmicort, 131
pulmonary vein, 16, 17
pulse, acute attacks, 96–8
purinergic system, 7

radial artery, 99

radioimmunoassay techniques (RAST), 38
records, patient, 118
reproterol, 45, 46, 61
respiratory pattern, acute attacks, 98
respiratory syncytial virus (RSV)
    bronchiolitis, 1, 4, 5, 95, 121
respiratory tract infections, 4, 48, 59, 63, 64,
    80
reticuloendothelial system, 75
review procedures, 117–18
rhinitis, 41, 69
rhonchi, 35–6, 98
rimiterol, 46, 61
Rotahaler, 47, 56, 59, 63, 100
RSV bronchiolitis, 1, 4, 5, 95, 121

salbutamol, 39, 62, 63, 102
    in acute attacks, 101
    dosage, 46, 61
    and exercise-induced
        bronchoconstriction, 90
    peak flow rates, 52, 60
    for younger children, 62
schools, 83–4, 118–19
secretions, 8
    bronchial lavage, 107
    clearance of, 78
    dehydration, 104
    lung collapse, 92
sedatives, 95, 102
side-effects: aminophylline, 54, 96
    theophylline, 53, 54
skin tests, 39–42, 40–1, 69, 70, 72
slow-release beta$_2$ stimulants, 52
slow-release theophylline, 52, 58, 59, 61, 92
sodium cromoglycate, 51, 54–5, 56, 57, 59
    bronchiectasis, 93
    exercise-induced bronchoconstriction,
        10, 11, 89
    indications, 55
    mode of delivery, 54, 55
    nocturnal asthma, 90
    reduction of therapy, 55
    for younger children, 62–3, 64, 67
spacer devices, 112
special schools, 83–4
Spinhaler, 54, 62
spirometry, 9, 20, 22, 26, 38
sputum, green, 92
squill, 85
Staphylococcus aureus, 92
steroids, 55–9, 112
    acute attacks, 58, 107–8
    allergen bronchial provocation, 42
    bronchiectasis, 93
    dosage, 57
    exercise-induced bronchoconstriction,
        10, 89
    and growth rates, 33, 34, 35
    in herbal remedies, 85

steroids (cont.)
    indications, 56
    lung function tests, 38
    and mechanical ventilation, 107
    nocturnal asthma, 90–2
    systemic, 57–9, 64, 67, 85, 89, 107
    topical, 55–7, 62–3, 67, 89
    for younger children, 63–4, 67
stramonium, 85
stress, 80, 83
sympathetic nervous system, 7
symptom diaries, 118
systemic steriods, 57–9, 64, 67, 85, 89, 107

tachycardia, 48, 96
tartrazine, 74
tents, oxygen, 103
terbutaline, 45, 46, 61
tests, 36–42, 99
theophylline, 52–4, 58
    acute attacks, 101
    dosage, 52–4
    exercise-induced bronchoconstriction,
        10, 89
    nocturnal asthma, 52, 91, 92
    side-effects, 53, 54
    for younger children, 61–2, 63, 64, 66
thromboxanes, 56
thrush, 56
topical steriods, 55–7, 62–3, 67, 89
total body plethysmography, 28, 58
total pulmonary resistance, 28, 29
trachea: diameter, 7
    physical examination, 98
tracheal/bronchial stenosis, 32
tremor, 48
trigger factors, 95
troleandomycin, 53
tropical eosinophilia, 38
tryptase, 12
tumours, mediastinal, 32

ultrasonic nebulizers, 12, 42, 60, 65, 105
unconsciousness, 95, 102
underdiagnosis, 31
upper respiratory tract infections, 4, 48, 59,
    63, 64, 80

vascular rings, 32
ventilator therapy, 106–7
    babies, 33
Ventolin, 130
venturi effect, 20
viral infections, 1, 4, 31, 69, 94, 95, 111
Vitalograph, 20
Volumatic device, 63, 112

water spirometers, 20
wheezing, 4, 13, 31, 32, 94, 109–10

wheezy bronchitis, 1, 5, 31, 109
whooping cough, 32, 33
worm infestation, 38
Wright's peak flow meter, 18

x-rays, chest, 92, 94, 95, 99
xylometazoline, 28

yoga, 86–7

Other titles in the Practical Problems in Medicine series

PRACTICAL MANAGEMENT OF ASTHMA
Timothy Clark, Professor of Thoracic Medicine and Dean, Guy's Hospital Medical School and **John Rees**, Consultant Physician in Thoracic Medicine and Clinical Tutor, Guy's Hospital Medical School

'This book must make essential reading for many doctors.' *Lancet*

Illustrated throughout with over 100 high-quality photographs and diagrams in colour and black-and-white.

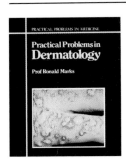

PRACTICAL PROBLEMS IN DERMATOLOGY
Ronald Marks, Professor of Dermatology, Welsh National School of Medicine

'This is an excellent book which I shall keep – and use – in my consulting room.' *British Medical Journal*

'This book is a good buy for the busy GP who wants to bring his dermatology up to date with the least possible effort.' *Current Practice*

Illustrated throughout with over 200 high-quality colour photographs and diagrams.

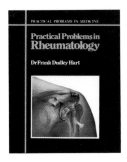

PRACTICAL PROBLEMS IN RHEUMATOLOGY
Frank Dudley Hart, Consultant Physician, Westminster Hospital

'This book, the first in a new series, will be a sure winner.' *Lancet*

Illustrated throughout with over 100 illustrations including specially commissioned artwork, full-colour photographs and many x-rays. Featuring a unique approach in the chapter on injection and aspiration where colour photographs and explanatory diagrams are given for each injection.

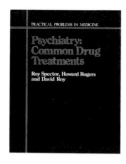

PSYCHIATRY: COMMON DRUG TREATMENTS
Roy Spector, Professor of Applied Pharmacology, Guy's Hospital Medical School; **Howard Rogers**, Reader in Clinical Pharmacology, Guy's Hospital Medical School and Consultant Physician, Guy's Hospital; **David Roy**, Consultant Psychiatrist, Goodmayes Hospital, and Senior Lecturer in Psychiatry, St Bartholomew's Hospital.

Based on many years' clinical and research experience, this book presents a clear, practical approach to the drug treatment of all psychiatric conditions commonly encountered in general practice. Illustrated with fifteen diagrams.

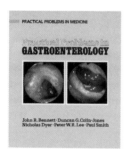

PRACTICAL PROBLEMS IN GASTROENTEROLOGY
General editor: **John R Bennett**, Consultant Physician, Hull Royal Infirmary, with **Duncan G Colin-Jones**, Consultant Physician, Queen Alexandra Hospital, Portsmouth, **Nicholas Dyer**, Consultant Physician, Worcester Royal Infirmary, **Peter W R Lee**, Consultant Surgeon, Hull Royal Infirmary, **Paul M Smith**, Consultant Physician, Llandough Hospital, South Glamorgan and the University of Wales College of Medicine, Cardiff.

'The greatest strength of this book lies in the detailed discussion of awkward symptoms of gastrointestinal disease'
Lancet

HYPERTENSION IN PRACTICE
D Gareth Beevers, Reader in Medicine, University of Birmingham and **Graham MacGregor**, Director of the Blood Pressure Unit, Charing Cross Hospital.

This title presents the causes and latest treatments for hypertension including both drug and non-drug methods of control. It will cover modern research aspects of hypertension only so that the reader will be equipped to start reading scientific articles on the subject in the major medical journals.

To be published:

PRACTICAL PROBLEMS IN ISCHAEMIC HEART DISEASE
Graham Jackson, Consultant Cardiologist, King's College Hospital
Publication: October 1987

OPHTHALMOLOGY IN MEDICINE: AN ILLUSTRATED CLINICAL GUIDE
J David Abrams, Consultant Ophthalmological Surgeon, Royal Free Hospital
Publication: October 1987

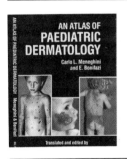

AN ATLAS OF PAEDIATRIC DERMATOLOGY
Carlo L Meneghini and **E Bonifazi**
Translated and edited by **Hilary Marks** and **Ronald Marks**

Aimed at postgraduate students in dermatology and paediatrics as well as primary care physicians.

Dentistry in Practice series
A unique illustrated dental series for practitioners and students

PLANNING AND MAKING CROWNS AND BRIDGES
Bernard G N Smith, Reader in Conservative Dentistry and Honorary Consultant, United Medical Dental School, Guy's Hospital

Detailed planning and longterm management of crowns and bridges have been neglected aspects of conventional teaching. Aimed at providing an understanding for undergraduates, postgraduates and dental practitioners, Dr Smith's clearly presented text provides comprehensive guidance on the realities that confront the practitioner in the surgery.

A further 5 titles to be published in 1988.